To Del,
I Know you wi
enjoy ♡
Dr. Jacqueline

MW01480730

WHY SHE *Stayed*

WHY SHE *Stayed*

BASED ON A TRUE STORY

JACQUALINE S BOLES

XULON PRESS

Xulon Press
2301 Lucien Way #415
Maitland, FL 32751
407.339.4217
www.xulonpress.com

© 2021 by Jacqualine S Boles

All rights reserved solely by the author. The author guarantees all contents are original and do not infringe upon the legal rights of any other person or work. No part of this book may be reproduced in any form without the permission of the author.

Due to the changing nature of the Internet, if there are any web addresses, links, or URLs included in this manuscript, these may have been altered and may no longer be accessible. The views and opinions shared in this book belong solely to the author and do not necessarily reflect those of the publisher. The publisher therefore disclaims responsibility for the views or opinions expressed within the work.

Unless otherwise indicated, Scripture quotations taken from the Holy Bible, New International Version (NIV). Copyright © 1973, 1978, 1984, 2011 by Biblica, Inc.™. Used by permission. All rights reserved.

Scripture quotations taken from the New King James Version (NKJV). Copyright © 1982 by Thomas Nelson, Inc. Used by permission. All rights reserved.

NOTE FROM AUTHOR:
This work depicts actual events in the life of the author as truthfully as recollection permits and/or can be verified by the memories of trusted individuals. Occasionally, dialogue consistent with the character or nature of the person speaking has been supplemented. All persons within are actual individuals; there are no composite characters. However, the names of some individuals have been changed to respect their privacy. Lord knows I've had enough drama in my life; I don't need anybody trying to sue me.

Paperback ISBN-13: 978-1-66283-169-0
Ebook ISBN-13: 978-1-66283-170-6

Dedication

I'd like to dedicate this book to all those who have suffered domestic violence and found their escape, you are true survivors!

And to those still suffering, it's not too late to get out. There's still hope.

Foreword

It was the winter of 1972, and it was certainly a harsh one, especially for my sister-in-law, Helen. She'd had a miscarriage the year before and the circumstances said she was about to have one again. I arrived to the house and there was a lot of blood, too much blood to comfort one's soul.

My brother, James, walked past me, "Well, she's lost another baby."

In that moment I was overcome, not by grief or sorrow but determination. I grabbed a sheet and went to work. Over the leg, between the legs, up the back of the other, between the legs again. Around and around until there was no sheet left. Then I took towels and packed them between her legs. "This baby is staying in you!" I declared and off we went to the hospital.

I'm sure that doctor thought we were crazy when we showed up with this woman in a giant sheet diaper. But after examining her, he looked at us with shock and informed us that although she'd hemorrhaged greatly and had lost a lot of blood, but the baby was still in the womb!

This was wonderful news, yet the miracle we had hoped for had not yet come to pass. The doctor told my sister-in-law she would need to stay in bed the rest of the pregnancy. Her cervix was in such critical condition that even getting up and going to the bathroom could potentially cause her to lose the baby.

I knew what had to be done. For the next three months, I took her into my house and cared for her. I cooked, I cleaned, I bathed her, and helped her use the restroom. I was determined that she would not lose another baby. And she didn't! On June 9th, my beautiful niece, Jackie, was born. She was a full-term healthy baby.

Here I thought that was an amazing testimony for her life. Little did I know God would use her life to reach even more people than I could ever imagine.

-Aunt Annie

Acknowledgments

To my beautiful parents. James and Helen Hicks, God rest them.

To my sisters, Angie and Missy, and my aunts, Annie and Flo. If it wasn't for your support and care, I don't know that I would be here.

To my husband, Dr. Lawrence C Boles, III and son Freddie Christopher, words cannot express my love and gratitude for the two of you in my life.

And to everyone else that I know but have not specifically named, God knows how you touched my life.

Table of Contents

Introduction xiii

Chapter 1: Love at First Sight 1

Chapter 2: Clarksdale, Mississippi 11

Chapter 3: Escape Strategy 15

Chapter 4: The Boyfriend 23

Chapter 5: Baby Bumps & Diamond Rings 33

Chapter 6: One Life to Live 39

Chapter 7: Mrs. Leonard & The Memphis Run 47

Chapter 8: Downhill to Destruction 53

Chapter 9: A Damaged Ego 63

Chapter 10: Welcome to the Circus 71

Chapter 11: Where's Sarena? 79

Chapter 12: The Monster & The Kidnapping 87

Chapter 13: Moving On 95

Chapter 14: A Good Man 103

Chapter 15: Lessons Along the Way 111

Chapter 16: That's Why She Stayed 121

Introduction

A woman stands at her kitchen sink doing dishes trying to remove the last remains of food from a skillet when yelling takes her attention away from the task. *Are they seriously at it again?* She sighs as she shuts off the water and leans forward just a bit. Although the blinds are closed next door, she can see through the area where they are broken. She leans forward a bit just to get a better look. Sure enough, she's already begun shaking her head and waving her finger in his face. *Oh dear, not again.*

"What is all that racket?" her husband's question almost makes her slip into the sink.

"Shh," she waves her hand at him, "it's the neighbors."

"Are you kidding me? I just put the kids to bed. They better not wake them up" He steps up beside his wife and leans towards the window looking for the same break in the miniblinds. "I swear, it's always something over there."

She continues to stare at the couple arguing, almost memorizing as she wonders, *How, can anyone live like that? Why does she even stay with that fool?*

Just then, the husband grabs hold of her wagging finger. She jerks away from him and pushes her hands against his chest. Now she's slapping him, he's blocking her hands and they're both screaming.

"I'm calling the police." She states dryly as she dries off her hands.

"What?"

"I'm calling the police." She repeats as she pulls her cell phone from her back pocket.

"Babe, it's not like we don't argue."

"But you were just saying how loud they were."

"Right, right but maybe we should just let them handle their business. They usually settle down after a while. I mean, would you want someone calling the police on us if we were arguing."

"We don't argue like that."

Her husband shrugs his shoulders. "I mean, everybody's different. As long as you kiss and make up at the end of the day, is it really a problem?"

She cocks her head to the side and raises her eyebrow. "If you *ever* yelled at me and got in my face like that," she says pointing to the window, "you can be sure I'd call 911." She goes back to scrubbing her skillet except this time a little bit faster. "I'd have to cause you'd need an ambulance after I hit you upside the head with this pan."

He laughs, wraps his arms around her waist, and sets his head on her shoulder. "Which is why I've never yelled at you like that."

After kissing her neck, her husband walks out of the room. The woman stops scrubbing for a moment and listens to the yelling. She shakes her head and goes back to scrubbing. "I do not understand why she stays with him."

WHY ON EARTH WOULD YOU STAY?

+++

According to the National Coalition Against Domestic Violence, "On average, nearly 20 people per minute are physically abused by an intimate partner in the United States. During one year, this equates to more than 10 million women and men."[1]

In the same year, the (CDC) National Center for Injury Prevention and Control, Division of Violence Prevention released their National Intimate Partner and Sexual Violence Survey 2010 Summary Report. The report covered 124 pages of statistics regarding domestic violence. On page 54 of the report, they listed out various forms of physical violence individuals received by an Intimate Partner in their lifetime, some of the forms included:

- 36,164,000 victims said they were slapped, pushed, or shoved.
- 8,403,000 victims were kicked by their intimate partner.

[1] National Coalition Against Domestic Violence. Statistics. https://www.ncadv.org/statistics

- 11,605,000 victims said their partner tried to hurt them by choking or suffocating them.
- 5,519,000 victims said their partner used a gun or knife on them.[2]

Do these numbers seem as crazy to you as they do to me? We're talking about millions of victims experiencing domestic violence. Looking at these numbers some people might think, "How does this happen?" Others might wonder, "What can be done?" But almost everyone would tend to wonder, when you're experiencing this kind of treatment from someone who should be showing you love and compassion, WHY ON EARTH WOULD YOU STAY?

And just like the couple at the beginning of the introduction, some of us disregard domestic abuse as none of our business. Every couple has their disagreements, right? Every couple raises their voice from time to time, right? How do we then determine when there might be something worse at play? Should we even try to determine if the couple may need outside intervention to handle?

It's always easier to judge somebody when you're standing on the sidelines of their situation. But what happens when you're in the middle of the fire and you don't even realize you're being burned to death? I am a survivor of multiple relationships involving domestic violence. I've witnessed belittling,

---

2 National Intimate Partner and Sexual Violence Survey 2010 Summary Report. November 2011. Page 54. *National Center for Injury Prevention and Control, Division of Violence Prevention* https://www.cdc.gov/violenceprevention/pdf/nisvs_report2010-a.pdf

manipulation, been held at gunpoint, and was even exposed to a murderer.

I can't speak for all the other women who've gone through domestic abuse but let me tell you WHY I STAYED.

Chapter 1

Love at First Sight

Is there really, truly such a thing as "love" at first sight? We may experience "ain't he fine" at first sight but I don't know that love is something we can instantly experience in a moment between a man and a woman.

I was raised in a pretty strict home, the baby daughter of a Pentecostal preacher. When I say "strict" I mean, you don't smoke, no red polish, don't even think about going to house parties, and especially no drinking alcohol. No, no, no, none of that nonsense. This might have made more sense to me if I didn't have "unsaved" aunts and uncles. They didn't go to church so the rules in their houses weren't as strict as mine. When I went to visit my cousins, I could listen to "worldly" music and watch Soultrain. Oh yeah, now that was fun! How come we couldn't have fun like this at home?

Being a preacher's daughter felt like I was living in a fish bowl. I couldn't do anything without it getting back to my parents. Which is why, when I graduated Garfield High School in

Seattle, Washington, I headed to Hampton University 3000 miles away! My plan was to have fun while I was at college; the last thing I needed was my parents being able to drive up just to say hello. Nope, that wasn't happening! If they wanted to come and visit me, they'd have to fly which meant they'd have to tell me they were coming to town.

I pledged to a sorority and had a ball! We'd hop in my car and drive all over the East Coast. I gained my freedom and lots of friends. My initial plan was to meet someone in college and get married after graduation. I dated someone while I was in college but nothing came of it. So here I was graduating from college and single. All I could think was, "Oh shoot, I'm not married."

I don't think this is something specific to me, I feel like the dream of being a wife bounces around in the fantasies of most little girls. You go to school, you go to college, and you get married. I mean, you've got to get married if you want to have the babies, right? At least, that is what you're taught in a preacher's home. I told my parents I didn't have any plans to return to Seattle but the truth was I didn't have any plans at all. I just wanted to continue having my freedom and live my life. It didn't take long for them to pack me up and take me back to Seattle.

> Women think they need a man to complete them. The truth is, only God can satisfy this desire in our soul. When we seek this from another human being, we will always feel a void.

I got back to Seattle and dated a few different guys but still, the relationships didn't go anywhere. The years seemed to be passing and I started getting a little nervous. I was 25, then I was 26 and I still hadn't locked down a husband. I needed to hurry up and do something! Around this time, a sorority sister from Seattle told me about her boyfriend's cousin, Mark. He had moved to Seattle from Atlanta, Georgia where he'd graduated from Morehouse College. Or at least that's what I was told. He'd just attended there, but he never graduated.

He had told his cousin he was interested in meeting somebody. My friend and his cousin hooked us up and I was immediately fascinated by him. We began dating and I became even more smitten by him. I went to Mississippi with him to meet his family; they were the sweetest people—his mother, sisters, aunts, and uncles. And best of all, my family was crazy about him. Which was great news for someone in a family as tight as mine. He always knew how to have a good time and instantly became the life of the party. The reason he was so loose and ready to have a good time was because alcohol was his best friend. I knew that Mark drank but I never would have considered him to have a drinking problem or be an alcoholic. In my mind, alcoholics were people who couldn't hold a job because of their addiction to booze. They were the ones who ended up bums on the street. I had no idea someone could be a functioning alcoholic.

The day finally came when Mark proposed. Of course, I said yes and we immediately began planning our wedding. A lot of my friends had gotten married or were getting married around that same time. Of that bunch of women, I think two of them are still married. And do you want to know why? Because the rest of us were getting married for all the wrong reasons. I can honestly say that I didn't even love Mark. I was so in love with what I thought marriage should look like that I never considered if I would truly enjoy spending the rest of my life with this man.

I grew up in this Cosby Show illusion of what life should be. Everybody's happy, everybody takes care of themselves. We were like the Huxtables, only Pentecostal. We all had cars when we were 16 years old and life was always very well put together. I thought that was how things would continue when I married Mark. He had a job; I had a job. We both were ready to contribute to our future together, right? Oh, was I fooled!

It took us a year of planning before we got to our wedding day. That felt like the longest year of my life! Our wedding was a big societal event, my parents did not hold back at all. My father rented 10 Lincoln Town cars for the groomsmen when they came into town. We had 18 bridesmaids and 18 groomsmen in the bridal party, it was huge! And the reception was to be held at the Sheraton's Grand Ballroom.

In the time leading up to the wedding, I, of course, had some people question whether or not I wanted to go through with the wedding. You see it happen all the time on TV shows and movies. There always seems to be people who have to ask the question, "Are you sure?"

Or sometimes there are people who get jealous, you found your man and they're still looking for theirs. Or worse, they wanted yours! None of that was the case when it came to the people who questioned me. These people were trying to warn me only I was oblivious to their concerns. One of the people I remember trying to talk me out of it was his cousin. She said, "Jackie, there's some things you need to know about Mark."

I'm sure I rolled my eyes as if there was anything *she* could possibly tell me about my soon-to-be husband that I didn't already know. I asked, "What do I need to know?"

The message she was trying to get through was lost in all the riddles and circles she spun through. Never once did she come right out and tell me exactly what I needed to know. She simply said, "He's always borrowing money from me."

I guess she assumed I would know what that meant but I had no clue what she was trying to tell me. I knew in my gut she was truly trying to warn me about something but I brushed it off. I'd already bought the wedding gown, we'd paid for the wedding, I'd reached the point of no return, there was no backing out. Whatever it was we could face it together, that's what married couples did, right?

Another person who tried to warn me was my twin cousin. I always called her this because we were just two months apart in age. She was one of the bridesmaids in my wedding. When I met up with her days before the wedding she said, "Jackie, you don't need to marry him."

"Why would you say that?" I asked, completely taken aback from her statement, "We're getting ready to have all these people come in for the wedding."

She said, "There's something you don't know."

That was the extent of our conversation that day. As I was working on this book, I called her up and said, "Remember when you told me I didn't need to marry Mark? Why'd you do that?"

She replied, "'Cause it was all over town that he was on drugs and I didn't want you mixed up in that."

I said, "What?! You guys knew about it and you never came out and told me?"

She said, "Jackie, you were so starstruck that you wouldn't have listened to us even if we *did* tell you."

And you know what, she was absolutely right. It was two weeks before the wedding and I was beginning to have some doubts. Mark had got into a habit of asking me, every day, if he could borrow $20. He'd always have a valid reason anytime I asked so other than getting a little annoyed I didn't think much else about it. I did wonder how our finances might be when we got married if he was always wanting to borrow some money but I brushed it off. I wasn't about to say anything. My parents had spent over $30,000 on this wedding, I couldn't turn back now.

But the one that should have thrown up the biggest flag, of all the people who tried to warn me, was my father. As we were standing there waiting for the doors to open so he could escort me down the aisle—600 people waiting inside—he looked at me and said, "Are you sure you want to do this?"

I said, "Yes, Daddy" And I never once asked him why he had asked me that.

We said, "I do." and it was done. I knew we'd be together for the rest of our lives. We had our elegant reception at the Sheraton ballroom and then we had a second reception at a private club. Despite everything my parents had put into the wedding, Mark insisted that he wanted to have a party reception with dancing and drinking. I told him I couldn't expect my parents to pay for something like that, I was a preacher's daughter. They weren't going to allow a DJ and drinking.

He simply replied, "Then, we'll have two."

+++

We had a honeymoon suite to stay in at the Sheraton Hotel then plans to fly out to our honeymoon in Florida two days later. But the night at the Sheraton was when all my dreams fell apart. I heard a strange sound and when I sat up to see what was going on, there was Mark with his head down to a table snorting a line of cocaine. My heart dropped into my shoes. I threw back the covers and said, "What are you doing?"

He said, "Oh, just a little coke, everybody snorts. It's called recreational."

My head was spinning as I jumped out of the bed. "What do you mean '*everybody* snorts?'" I objected, "Lots of people smoke marijuana not snort cocaine!"

He said, "It's alright I'm not addicted."

Tears welled up in my eyes. I wasn't sure which was worse, my anger or embarrassment. How could I have married someone who snorted cocaine? How did I not see this sooner? I was livid, this was not the kind of marriage I had signed up for. My parents had taken all the gifts back to their house so the plan was to meet the family at their house for breakfast and open our gifts. As I got dressed, reality was weighing on me—I couldn't tell anyone what I had woken up to this morning. I got dressed and put a smile on with my clothes. Nobody needed to know anything about the honeymoon suite or the cocaine. We were a happily married couple and that's all they needed to know.

And that was when my acting career began!

The next day, we caught a plane to Florida for our honeymoon. If I had to compare my wedding and honeymoon to desserts here is how it would go: the wedding day was like I had been given my own individual cake created by a world-class baker who delicately placed white chocolate on the cake in such a way it looked as if the cake had been covered in lace. It was intricately thought out and wonderfully presented, absolutely fabulous. But the honeymoon, on the other hand, was like someone had left a Twinkie on the dash of their car, it flew out the window, they drove over it, and then handed me the smushed up contents with a smile and said, "Enjoy." Oh, it was worse than awful!

Mark was broke! Which made the honeymoon awful because I had to pay for everything. Here I am pulling out cards, "Oh we're on our honeymoon, aren't we so happy?"

I had my suspicions that he was a poor manager of money but I thought love would fix that. If he loved me then he would do right by me. You know what the worst part about having an awful cocaine snorting husband is? Returning home and not being able to complain about any of it. How could I? My family all thought he was great. And I won't say divorce was unheard of in my family but it was certainly a taboo topic. When someone gets married, they stick with it for the long haul. The last thing I needed was to tell them I'd married the wrong man. My father was a prestigious pastor within the community, I didn't want to embarrass my parents or bring any shame to the family. No, we were going to make this work; I was determined!

When we got married, I was in college working on getting my masters. I used this to keep my mind off Mark's habit. Even though he never snorted in front of me again I knew that his $20 a day habit hadn't gone away. During the course of the next year, he kept getting fired and couldn't hold a job. Whenever he would get hired, he'd end up failing the drug test. Despite his lack of income, he continued to party and drink. Every once in a while, things go missing because he ends up pawning them to keep up with his habit. I did my best to keep up with him but the façade was wearing on me. I confided in my sister that things weren't as good as I was making them out to be. I was paying all the bills and our marriage was awful. But still, we were in Seattle, so I still felt the need to pretend things were going well for the sake of my family.

Chapter 2

Clarksdale, Mississippi

After I graduated in June 1999, I decided that I could no longer keep up with the façade. I told Mark we should move to Mississippi and try living around his family. His family was ecstatic. Mark was back in their hometown and his new wife Jackie was there to take care of him. His mother never came out and said it but I could tell by the way she acted that she knew her son needed someone to take care of him.

I had a great career as a nurse practitioner. I met his god-sister, who was also a nurse practitioner and we instantly became close. She began hinting that my husband had a drug problem. But I was still in denial. I knew he had issues because once again things started to turn up missing. I didn't realize he was pawning things again because it was tools from the shed and things like that at first. I knew he had a problem with drugs but I wasn't willing to admit it to anyone. As far as I was concerned, it was an issue we'd work through.

The only problem now was that we lived in the small rural town of Clarksdale, Mississippi where everybody knew everybody. Everyone knew what everybody was up to and what everybody was doing so it didn't take long for word of Mark's drug addiction to spread around town. It didn't matter who tried to tell me though, I wouldn't hear of it. As far as I was concerned, they were all jealous.

We had a home on a half-acre of land with a swimming pool. We'd throw the biggest parties where we'd supply all the food and liquor. Sometimes I would even have the food catered. That was our life and our marriage, one big party.

The one thing that I looked forward to and dreaded twice a year was a visit from my parents. They were a part of a Pentecostal organization called Church of God in Christ. The organization hosted two large conventions each year at their headquarters which was located in Memphis, Tennessee. Memphis was only an hour from Clarksdale so every time they came down for their convention, they'd stop by to see us. I loved seeing them but dreaded being asked, "Are you ok? How are you doing?"

Mark was an excellent performer. He'd put on such a show of how good things are that he even had me convinced, although I knew it wasn't true. I hated lying to my parents but I still felt it was necessary to keep up the façade. They'd stay at our house in the guest room and for those three or four days everything in our life would be sunshine and roses.

Around year three is when things got rough. We had a beautiful black lab named Ebony. I only fed her canned dog food.

Yes, she was spoiled, but the vet said it kept her coat pretty. I got home one day and the brand-new box of dog food was gone.

"Mark, where's the dog food?" I asked as I looked through the house.

"Oh, I took it back to the store."

"Took it back to the store? Why?"

"Well, it had worms in it?"

"There were worms in the dog food?"

"Yeah."

"Well, what did you do with the money?" Never once did I ask how worms had gotten into all the *cans* of dog food.

"Oh, I needed it for gas."

That was how he was, he always had a quick lie for everything. And I better not dare leave a receipt lying around the house because I would never see what I had bought again and certainly wouldn't get the money. Still, I continued to be determined to make our marriage work. Even when I came home from work and flipped the switch, but nothing happened. I thought maybe the power had gone out but I could see out the window the neighbors had power. When I called the electric company, they informed me that I hadn't paid my bill. I assured her that I had given the money to my husband to pay the bill but she told me they'd not received any money. That began happening more frequently. I'd give him money to pay a bill, it would never get paid, and he would have the grandest story as to why it hadn't got paid and why he didn't have the money.

It was all too much. Finally, I sat him down and told him we needed to have a heart to heart. "Mark, I'm not happy. Things have got to change if we want this marriage to continue."

"What do you mean?" he asked, completely oblivious of any issues, "Aren't you happy?"

"Happy?" I shook my head in disbelief, "No, I'm not happy. I'm paying all the bills. You won't come home at night and if you do you are drunk."

After this he became verbally abusive. If I didn't give him his $20 each day, he'd cuss me out and call me all kinds of names. I started sleeping with my purse under my pillow because I would wake up and money would be gone out of my purse. We were on the same bank account and he would constantly be overdrawing and taking out money every time I got paid. My friend, his god-sister, told me I should get him off the bank account because he was going to ruin my credit if we stayed on an account together. So, I went to the bank to have him removed. While I was at the bank, he came storming into the bank and went ballistic. He was blaming his god-sister for taking him off the account. As if I didn't have a mind of my own! The banker told him he needed to leave.

Once again, let me remind you that we're in a small rural town. So, of course, this became the talk of the town. When he walked into the bank that day, he literally looked like a bum. He hadn't shaved, his beard wasn't trimmed, and he had been wearing the same clothes for three days. He was really starting to look like an addict.

Chapter 3

Escape Strategy

Sometime during the fourth year of our marriage I began planning my exit strategy. I had to get out; I had to get away from Mark. A friend of mine had told me, "Jackie, you can't compete with that female called cocaine. She is worse than any woman trying to get your man from you." And she was right! There was nothing he would not do or sacrifice to get his fix. He'd threaten me multiple times and one time nearly ran me over all because I wouldn't give him money for his fix. He had made it perfectly clear that he would never give up his "snow-white mistress" as I had come to know it. He even justified himself by saying, "I don't smoke crack, I do cocaine." I'm not sure how that was supposed to make me feel better.

I tried telling his mother that Mark was on drugs but she was in even more denial than me. "Who's making him do them?"

"What do you mean, 'who's making him do it?'" I shook my head in disbelief. I was 30 years old; Mark was 36. How can anyone MAKE a grown adult do drugs? There are many times when the family is the worst enabler of an abuser, especially when they're in denial. His sister knew about his drug problem but she wouldn't dare say a word. She would try to correct him at times but he must have done something to scare her straight because eventually she stopped saying anything.

By this time, I had made up my mind about two things—I was leaving and I had to save money. I had a day job but I began picking up weekend nursing shifts as well. I started working at all kinds of different places mainly just to be away from the house so I wouldn't have to be bothered by him. Then one day I get a call at work. Mark has fallen off a horse and broken his leg. "What do you mean he's fallen off a horse? He's supposed to be at work."

I meet him at the hospital and he already has a story lined up. He's gotten a new job and they let him off early so he went to ride horses with a friend. Despite all our issues, I'm so naïve that I believe him. His leg was broken so badly that they had to transfer him from the hospital in our little town to one in Oxford, Mississippi. When we get there, an orthopedic surgeon puts pins and screws in his leg. After the surgery, he's sweating like crazy and telling me how much pain he's in. They keep bringing him painkillers, like enough pain killers that this man should have been knocked out yet he's still screaming and hollering.

"Just go to sleep." I said, trying to quiet him down. All the while, the real issue is that he's having withdrawals from cocaine.

"Jackie, call this person."

I had no idea why this person needed to be called but I called him anyway. When he showed up, Mark told me to give him $20. It wasn't until that moment that I realized this guy was his dealer. I had my own family practice. I had to take off work and have somebody cover my patients just to deal with his nonsense and now he wanted me to pay his dealer? It wasn't happening! When I refused to pay the man, he threw the bedside urinal at me, covering me in pee, and began cussing me out. That was the straw that broke the camel's back!

I looked straight at him and said, "You'll never do that again. I'm done with you." Then I called up his mother and said, "You come take care of your son because I'm divorcing him. I'm tired, I'm through, I'm done with this marriage."

She said, "What?"

So, I stated it again a little slower. "I said I'm done. I'm divorcing him."

I left him at the hospital, drove back to Clarksdale and got a hotel room. Even though I was the one paying all the bills, I refused to stay at the house with him. I made up my mind that we were going to get a divorce. He gets home from the hospital and his mother keeps asking me why I won't take care of my husband. She's in so much denial. The whole town is in an uproar of gossip, "Jackie left Mark and he's laid up in bed with a broken leg. How you gonna leave a man with a broken leg? Shame on you."

Then a story started circulating around town that I was leaving Mark because I wanted a baby. His family knew I had been taking fertility shots because I wanted to have a baby.

What they didn't know was that we had gone to a fertility specialist and discovered that I wasn't the problem. The report said his sperm was swimming backwards! Typically, they should be aggressive. When they come out the fight to get to the egg. His were messed up and sluggish because of the drugs. It didn't matter if I stood on my head, I wouldn't be getting pregnant by Mark. Well, his family thought that must be the reason I was leaving their golden boy so they spread it around town.

I didn't care what people thought, I've had all that I can take. And then, I find out there was never a horse. He owed his drug dealer money and when he couldn't pay up, they broke his leg. All the while, no one in my family back in Seattle knows what is going on in my life. I've coasted through the past four years acting like it's all good. While I was at the hotel, he asked if he could meet with me and talk. He started with his smooth talking and asked if I would stay with him if he went to rehab. For whatever reason, I decided I'd try this one last attempt to save our marriage. I called the rehab facility in Jackson, Mississippi, paid the deposit, and set everything up. Then I purchased a Greyhound ticket and said, "Ok, if you really want to do this, go catch the bus."

We're standing there at the station and he says, "Oh I'm not going anywhere."

I said, "What do you mean? The deposit is paid and everything is all set up. All you have to do is get yourself on the bus."

He refused, and that's when I knew I decided we were obsolete, no turning back, one hundred percent through. There was no way to help someone who didn't want to help themselves. At that point, I called my mother and said, "I'm done, it's a wrap."

I told her about everything he had put me through and that I was filing for divorce. She said, "Jackie, you get him a one-way ticket to Seattle, we're gonna do the rehab for him. We're gonna get him saved, we're gonna give him Jesus. Jesus is going to come into his life and we're gonna clean him up. We're gonna move him here to Seattle and he will get the Holy Ghost and when you see your husband, you're going to see a new creature."

> There is a stigma in Christianity about divorce. A lot of Christians would pull up the verse saying, "God hates divorce." Well, did he tell us to stay in abuse? I never read that verse.

My dad was not for this plan at all but there was no way he would go against my mother. So instead of telling her it was a bad idea he just stood back and let her take charge of "Project Mark." They helped him get an apartment and then they helped him get a job at a car rental company. My mother was an evangelist, and in the Pentecostal church they did something they called tarrying for the Holy Ghost. The person who needs the Holy Ghost gets on their knees and everyone else is clapping their hands and telling them to say, "Save me Jesus." So, that's what they decided to do with Mark, to receive the Holy Ghost. They're praying for him to get this devil out of him. And all the while he is there, she is reporting back to me and telling me, "Look how Mark's doing. Isn't he doing good?"

I said, "Mom, the man is an addict. He needs help from a professional rehab facility. All he's doing is fooling you. I will not take him back."

I filed for divorce thinking it would finally be over but that fool starts taking me through every level of hell. He contested the divorce and dug everything out—I want the bed, I want the dog, my mother gave you that table, —thank God we didn't have any children!

Mark's in Seattle, I'm back at my house, things seem to be going well. I'm moving forward with the divorce and then I meet somebody. But since my divorce isn't final yet and I'm still living in small-town Clarksdale I try to keep everything lowkey. We're just flirting, nothing serious. I went to Seattle for my father's family reunion and my mom set up a counseling session for us. The marriage counselor is trying to convince me to stay in my marriage, Mark is trying to convince me to stay in my marriage. All the family at our reunion is trying to tell me we can work things out. But when I began explaining what I had been through and why I was getting a divorce they were in shock. The gossip mill in Seattle seemed to be worse than the one in Clarksdale. I had people from my dad's church calling me up, asking why things weren't working out between me and Mark. I would explain myself to some people and others I wouldn't even waste my time. There were some that said, "You've been through all that and you stayed?" They couldn't believe it.

"You've been through all that and you stayed?"

For the most part, I did my best to avoid Mark. But then my mom had my sister take me to an RV park. She knew that I had been wanting to buy one. On the side of one of these RV's is a big poster that says: Mark's in love with Jackie. Will you take me back, please?

There was Mark, standing by the trailer, explaining that he had bought it. I knew he hadn't bought it; he was always broke! I saw the sign and got so upset I started crying. I turned to my mom and said, "Mom, you mean to tell me that you want me to stay with this man after everything I told you he's done to me?"

"But he's saved and clean and I done fixed him." she objected and then saw the tears in my eyes, "You really don't want him, do you?"

"No!" I hollered, "I have a boyfriend!"

I was so frustrated that she could not understand the five years of pain I had endured. But I also didn't blame her for not understanding because I hadn't told anybody. I never believed in pulling anyone into my roller coaster. It was my ride and I planned to suffer through it alone. There was never any physical abuse in our marriage but the emotional abuse had wreaked havoc.

Mark continued to drag everything out causing me more and more attorney fees until his god sister finally stepped in. She finally told him, "Unless you want all that you've done to come out in court—cause we're gonna tell it—you better sign those papers and let Jackie get on with her life."

So that's what he did and I closed that chapter of my life.

Chapter 4

The Boyfriend

You know, before I even begin telling you about this ***amazing*** man I met, let me start by saying the worst thing for a woman to do, no for anyone to do, is jump out of one relationship straight into another. And yet, I see people doing it all the time, "Oh but he's different." Yep, that's exactly what I thought about Leo.

Before Mark went off to Seattle, I had stayed in a hotel for two months. I kept all the bills paid because I had planned to move back into the house once I got rid of him. One night, I went to a friend's birthday party at a blues club called Ground Zero. It's a pretty popular place in Clarksdale because it's owned by Morgan Freeman and Bill Luckett. Mark showed up at the club, chasing me for $20. Thankfully, my girlfriend was my bodyguard. She warned me he was coming and I ignored him. He ended up leaving without any money. But on that night, I also met Leo. He was one of the security guys at the club. We were flirting and smiling with each other. He ended up walking me out to my car and asked if he could call me. I said ok and gave him my number.

> When you go through a breakup, surround yourself with people who will protect you so you don't throw yourself at the first man to give you attention.

This was the worst mistake I could have made, jumping straight from one relationship into another. I didn't realize I was like a deer in headlights; stumbling around in the darkness of my pending divorce when out of nowhere these lights shine on me. Here I thought it was the beautiful stars aligning only to realize it was an eighteen-wheeler named Leo about to destroy me. But here I am getting ahead of myself.

We met up on some backroads outside of town. We were talking and he asked me why I was so sad. I said, "I'm just tired of dealing with drug addicts." Then I fell on him and cried.

Of course, he didn't miss a beat. He swooped right in and said, "Why would he hurt you like this? I can't believe it. Nobody should do a woman like that. Give me a chance and I'll show you how you should be loved."

Oh, those words hooked me in.

Leo and Mark were complete opposites. Leo didn't have any issues with drugs whatsoever. And he was a manly man, he knew how to take care of things. The first time Leo came to my house, he noticed the brick stairs leading to the front door were broken. He asked, "How long has this been broken?"

"Oh, a long time."

"Well, they can be fixed."

"No, I don't have that kind of money right now." I told him.

"It won't cost much; I can fix it for you." And he did!

Oh man, did I think I had hit the jackpot with this man. We began hanging out more and I found out Leo had five children. (At least that is all I knew about at the time. It wasn't until much, much later, that I discovered he had two other children but was not open about them because their mother was a preacher's wife. So, in reality, he already had seven children.) Rather than detour me, this made me want to pursue him more. I had just turned 31 and my birth clock was ticking. Mark never gave me any babies but this guy has already proven he can get someone pregnant. Or rather four someone's in his case.

Don't judge me, just keep on reading!

One day, around April, I'm out at his house in the country watching a movie when we hear a car door shut followed by yelling and cussing. He jumped up and said, "Oh I know she is not here at my house."

I said, "Who?"

"Sarena." Was all he replied before walking out to "take care of" her.

I had heard about his ex-girlfriend, Sarena. Leo had told me she was pretty crazy and very possessive. As I stared out the window, I could feel my heart saying, "Get your keys and purse.

Leave this man right now. You don't need to bother with this kind of drama."

I'm sure it was actually the Holy Spirit trying to warn me. But I didn't listen. My mind immediately flipped to challenge accepted mode. I was like, "Oh no, you won't win here."

That's why you shouldn't jump from one relationship to the next. It puts you in a weak vulnerable state. I left a bad relationship and thought I had found a good replacement; nobody was going to mess with that!

She's out-front crying, "You're going to leave me and I'm pregnant."

"It's not my baby!" Leo objected and looked at her friend, "You need to take her out of here."

At this point she was begging him, "I don't care what I have to do, I'll share you with her. Please don't leave me."

I'm staring at this drama through the window thinking, *Share him? I'm not sharing anyone.*

She is a hysterical crying mess. Her friend is apologizing, "I didn't know she was going to do this. She told me she was going to pick some things up. Sarena, get in the car and let's go."

"I don't want to go." Sarena, cried, "I want Leo."

"I don't want you." Leo shook his head and walked back into the house, "That girl is crazy. I don't want her."

I stared at him for a moment, "Dude if you're not done with all that..." I waved toward the window, "...then let me know now. Because I'm coming out of a bad marriage and I don't want this."

"Oh no, I promise, this will never happen again. She will never bother us again."

And just like that he hooked me in once again with some kind of voodoo magic. He was the best man in the world and he could do no wrong.

What's Mine is Yours

After this insanity with Sarena, I decided I was going to commit to the relationship. I met his family and everybody liked me. We're all getting along and he asks me to join his church. Even though I wasn't walking with the Lord as I should have been, I was impressed that he wanted me to join his church. I left my Pentecostal church and joined his Baptist church. I never would have done this in the past but Leo had some kind of crazy love spell on me. I thought he was some amazing find so I was willing to do whatever needed to be done to impress him and keep him.

Sarena and him had been dating for five or six years. She was pretty close with his family and good friends with his sister Shirley. So even though they liked me they didn't naturally gravitate towards me. If anything, they saw dollar signs when I walked in. I did whatever he asked and whatever his family asked. If they needed to borrow money, if they needed a light bill paid, I had my own practice and I was living good so I took care of it. I even opened up my house to his family.

We met each other in February 2004. The Sarena drama happened somewhere around the beginning of April. At that time, my divorce was not yet final but May was right around the time when I sent Mark off to "rehab" with my mother. With

Mark out of the state, I felt like I could finally breathe. I could move on with my life. Leo and I started dating and even though we weren't sexual we were doing some hot and juicy kissing. He started spending the night, then he'd spend another night. I gave him a drawer to put some things in, told him to leave his toothbrush at the house, and before I knew it, I was handing him a key because he was at my house more than his own. After all, I had the big house with half an acre of land.

I went to my family reunion and then in July I was finally free of Mark. My divorce was final!

Shortly after Leo moved in on a more permanent basis, his daughter Avery asked if she could move in. Here I was the instant live-in girlfriend and somewhat step-mom yet my divorce wasn't even final. Down in the south everybody gets a handle, ma'am or sir, out of respect. I was "Mama Jackie" that's what his kids called me. My spare bedrooms were taken over from time to time by his nieces who had run away from home and needed somewhere to stay.

Aunt Flo Coming to Check on Me

Around the end of summer, my Aunt Flo came down for a visit. I had no idea that my mother had paid for my aunt to come visit because she wanted her to break me and Leo up. But when Aunt Flo got to Mississippi, she didn't see anything wrong. We were having barbecues and partying at the house with music and dancing. From everything that Aunt Flo observed, we were happy and he seemed like a nice guy. She was a little concerned that I might be moving too fast since we were already living together but she decided to keep that to herself.

By this time, Sarena and I were in an undeclared war. She was still telling everyone in town that she was pregnant with Leo's baby and I had stolen him from her. And the worst part was that everyone loved the drama. When my aunt came to town, Leo's daughter Avery, and his two nieces told my aunt they were going to show her where Sarena worked. She agreed to go with them since she was curious to see who this woman was that everyone was talking about. When they got to the clothing store where Sarena worked as a sales clerk, she called the police on my aunt! The police told her not to come to the store and bother Sarena.

She said, "I didn't, these girls brought me here. They told me she was pregnant and wouldn't leave Leo alone."

I had no idea they had gone to the store and was never told the full stories until just recently. But when they came home the girls were all the buzz, "Sarena called the police on Auntie Flo and we just went up there to show her who she was."

In that moment, I sat on Leo's lap and said, "Leo, is this true? Is this girl really pregnant by you?"

He said, "No, she's just obsessed with me."

Then I began to laugh. I don't remember this conversation at all but my Aunt Flo remembered it in great detail because she was caught off guard by how blinded I was.

Leo got on the phone right in front of us and told Sarena off. He told her not to bother him, or me, or my aunt and mind her own business. That just made my day when he did that.

He's a Dangerous Guy

While Aunt Flo was in town, we decided to take her to Ground Zero. Once again, Sarena found us and started up her drama. I saw her walking up out of the corner of my eye. She got to Leo and asked, "Why do you keep ignoring me? I'm pregnant with your baby."

"It's not my baby." Leo replied, trying to brush her off. No sooner had she left the club then his phone rings. It's his sister Shirley, wondering why he won't talk to Sarena when she's pregnant with his baby. "I told her it's not mine. I don't know why you keep bothering me, it's not my baby."

With the drama finally settled we decided to visit with Leo's friend Tyler. He was the DJ for the club and lived above the apartment. As we were sitting around talking, Leo and Tyler started dreaming up plans about getting a food truck.

I piped up and said, "I'll be an investor."

> Desperate to please, is the worst place a woman can be.

Tyler walked out of the room with my Aunt during that conversation. I never thought too much about it that night but recently my Aunt told me that he was trying to warn her. He said, "Your niece is moving too fast. Leo is a dangerous guy to play with."

She told him, "Oh, ok I'll let her know." But she never said anything to me about the conversation because she wasn't really sure what he had meant by "*dangerous guy*." She thought, at the time, he just meant it was reckless to throw money at someone I hadn't been dating very long.

Chapter 5

Baby Bumps and Diamond Rings

October was the first time I actually saw Sarena's baby bump. Well, it was more than that by then, she was really, really pregnant. She was trick-or-treating with her daughter and a few other kids near my neighborhood. I walked into the house and informed Leo, "Sarena really is pregnant. I just saw her."

For a moment, he had the strangest look on his face but then replied, "Well, it ain't mine."

By this time, I had been getting earfuls from his sister Shirley, "That baby is *so* his, you'll see when it's born."

I looked at him and said, "According to your sister it is yours."

He called her up and asked why she kept telling me the baby was his. He told her to mind her own business and leave me alone. I didn't see how that would happen since she worked at my practice. Everything was wearing on me. By this time, we'd been together eight months and none of the gossip about

Sarena's pregnancy was slowing down. Then, I came home from shopping one day to find a boy in Avery's room. I told her it was time for her to go live with her mom because I couldn't deal with that kind of drama. She wasn't about to get pregnant on my watch. I'm sure Leo could tell I was slipping away with every question I asked.

"You told me she wasn't pregnant but I saw her and she is clearly pregnant. Your sister and mom are both telling me she's pregnant, what's going on Leo? Is this your baby?"

The last thing a liar wants is to be confronted with the truth. It was at that moment when he did what any manipulative man who wants the upper hand might do, he proposed.

I'm Getting Married

It was Christmas and he called up his family, "I just asked Jackie to marry me and she said yes."

I hadn't even been divorced a year. I don't know what business I thought I had getting into another marriage but I was elated to have one up on Sarena. He had never proposed to her. Ladies, let it be known, if you're excited to have "one up" on the ex-girlfriend, you may want to do some severe evaluation of your relationship. Shirley was having a birthday party around this time and I walked in showing off my ring. Sarena was there and she began crying hysterically. I know I must have had the biggest grin on my face as I thought, *Yeah, you only thought you had him.*

I know I was just awful to think such a thing but those are the kind of games women play when their self-esteem is broken. They want to be accepted and flaunt the ring showing who accepted them.

Baby Mama Drama

Sometime in January, the phone rings, it's his sister Shirley, "We have a new addition to the family."

He replied, "I told you it wasn't mine."

I'm not sure how I stayed as naïve as I did for as long as I did but I asked, "Why is she calling to tell you this baby is born?"

He continues to argue with her on the phone until she tells him that she named the baby Leo. When I heard this, I threw my hands up, "I'm so through. She named this baby after you and you're still saying it's not yours? Even your sister is saying it's your baby."

Leo stormed out of the house furious over the matter. He came back later apologizing. He kept assuring me that he didn't understand why she kept saying the baby was his. He knew, for sure, that it wasn't. About three or four weeks go by and his sisters, he had four of them, decided to go see the baby. Shirley called me that day and said, "Jackie, I don't know why he won't stop lying to you. I saw the baby and it is his."

I was absolutely crushed. Here I was getting married to this man and I wasn't even sure what to believe. He was adamant that it wasn't his and everyone else in town is convinced that it is! In that moment, I wanted to cut my losses and get out before things got worse. I didn't want to deal with this drama for the rest of my life. But Leo begged me not to leave him, so I stayed.

She Poisoned Me!

Sometime at the beginning of February, I got really sick. I was throwing up; my head was pounding. For whatever reason, I became convinced that Sarena had somehow poisoned me. I called my sister and began telling her my symptoms. I'm a nurse practitioner; why couldn't I figure out how to fix myself?

My sister laughed at my dilemma, "Oh you're just pregnant."

I couldn't believe she would say such a thing. Could that really be the case? I stopped taking my birth control after I got engaged because Aunt Flo told me it might take a while to get out of my system. I'd only had sex that one time on New Year's Eve when things got a little crazy passionate. Surely, I couldn't be pregnant.

"Girl, you're pregnant." She replied in that heartless yet caring way only a sister can deliver truth.

I went to the store and bought four different pregnancy tests. A $20 one, a $7 one, a $2 one, and even one from the dollar store. All four came back positive! The initial shock was replaced with excitement. I was finally pregnant! Mark and I had tried for years to get pregnant and were not successful but here Leo got me pregnant on the first try! I called my sister back and told her she was right. Then, I called my parents. They weren't quite as excited. My father said, "You need to get married; you can't have this baby out of wedlock."

I didn't see any problem with that, after all, we were already engaged. But when I told Leo he didn't see things the same way. "I was just proposing I'm not ready yet."

I couldn't believe it. He gave me a ring, he proposed, but he wasn't ready to get married yet? Even though I was pregnant with his baby? It was such a devastating blow, and yet, I continued to stay with him. Now, I felt even more trapped, this time by my shame. I was engaged, I got pregnant, and I couldn't walk away.

He's Mine!

Sarena was always around at family events and I absolutely hated it. So, when Shirley was telling me at work that Sarena wanted to bring the baby over for Easter dinner at her parents' house, I immediately called Leo. I guess he called Shirley and told her not to have Sarena come over. There was my one-up once again. I always felt accomplished when I shut Sarena down.

Then, right before Easter, I'm driving home from work and got a call from Shirley. She said, "Come out to mom's house. There's somebody you need to see."

When I got to her mom's house, there were a lot of people at the house. I thought it was strange, even Leo was there. I walked in and Shirley said, "Jackie, Sarena's baby is here."

> Every single day was a soap opera,
> and Shirley was the director!

I know everybody is posting nowadays: Don't be a Karen. Honey, don't be a Shirley! This woman thrived on drama! I looked at Leo, "How did this baby get here?"

He replied, "I brought him here. Sarena wanted me to show him to mom and dad."

I said, "So it ***is*** your baby?"

He looked at me and said, "Yeah, he's mine."

I started crying hysterically. His words crushed me. So, he really did impregnant Sarena weeks before we started dating, then he spent the last year lying to me? I was beside myself. His mother, who was always very calm, said, "You mean you didn't tell Jackie you were bringing the baby here?"

Shirley didn't miss a beat in her dramatic script, "Jackie, you need to get over yourself. This baby is a part of the family and you need to accept that. Just like your baby will be a part of this family too."

I managed to calm down enough to pick up the baby. I wanted to know for myself. And when I looked at that baby's face, I knew it was Leo's baby, no doubt in my mind. I shook my head in disbelief, this was really how things were going to be. He left to take the baby home and I went back to my house. When he got back to the house, we had a huge fight. He stormed out of the house and I went to stay with my friend. I was hurt and mad. I could not believe this was my life.

Chapter 6

One Life to Live

It was in that moment; I unknowingly became the lead in the most dramatic soap opera anyone could ever have imagined. My fiancé, his ex-girlfriend, her baby, and me—the pregnant lady along for the ride. The worst part was I was blind to how much control I had given this drama in my life. Leo's sister Shirley was my office manager, so I saw her every day at work. And I already told you she was the one flipping all the switches on the drama board. She knew how to light it up faster than anyone I know.

Leo's family always loved having big cookouts for holidays and pretty much any event they could have an excuse to get together. Since Shirley was my office manager and her daughter worked at the front desk, we found ourselves discussing the next holiday on the agenda—Mother's Day. The family always discussed where it would be and who would bring what. As we were talking about this Shirley suddenly says, "Well, Leo says he is going to cook for *all* the mothers."

I said, "All the mothers?"

Shirley said, "Yeah, me, my sisters, mom, you know everybody that's a mother."

"Oh, ok." I replied thinking it was sweet of him to volunteer.

We decided to have the cookout at his parents' house which was right next door to Leo's house. They lived out in the country so you could see the road and anyone who was pulling up. We're all outside laughing, listening to music, and having a good time; when out of the corner of my eye I catch sight of a golden Chevy Tahoe. That SUV might as well have been an army tank because every time I saw it, I knew war was about to break loose.

Leo's daughter ran up to the vehicle, "Oh, Sarena, you brought little Leo." She was all excited to see her brother. Not me, about that time I know I had fire in my eyes. I turn around and I said, "I'm not staying here for this." And retreated to Leo's house.

Shirley, of course, came knocking on the door, "Jackie?"

"I can't believe you invited her."

"It wasn't me Law." Shirley liked calling me law, short for sister-in-law even though we weren't married yet. "Maybe mama told her to stop by and get a plate. Come back out here you making Leo upset."

Looking back, there must have been a slew of demons at work that day because the tension was so thick you could cut it with a knife. I decided to stand by Leo as he barbequed the food. I remember his daughter coming and asking Leo if he wanted to hold the baby. Leo said no since he was cooking.

Sarena looked around and said, "I just came by to get a plate."

Shirley said, "I'll fix it for you."

I found it very hard to believe that Shirley hadn't been the one to invite her. His sweet mother didn't seem to know what was taking place and his dad kept saying, "Jackie, she just came by to get a plate, it's ok."

She didn't stay more than twenty minutes tops. As the golden SUV drove off in the distance, I once again felt as if I had experienced a victory. I got my way. He stayed with me and she had to leave. One on the board for me.

A Taste of Psycho

Sometime in June, I came home from work and found my house in shambles. The sheets were pulled off the beds, dishes were broken, the ribbons were pulled from the VHS tapes, including the baby's ultrasound. I couldn't figure out why someone would break into the house and destroy it, even punched a hole in the wall. Just then, Leo walked in. I started telling him I wasn't sure if someone broke into the house and he said, "I tore up the house."

I said, "Why did you tear up the house?"

Then he went on a rant about me thinking I was going to leave him. He went on and on about me and my friend sneaking around seeing other men. Then he told me he hated me and couldn't believe I was trying to leave him. I wasn't even sure what to say, he was completely delusional. I had gone to a pharmaceutical rep dinner where the salespeople take you to a fancy restaurant to present their new products. Everyone at the dinner was a professional colleague and he thought I was gallivanting with some man.

I remember his oldest son coming into the house and saying, "Dad, what's wrong with you? Aren't you happy you have Jackie?"

Leo stormed off and, in that moment, I realized this must have been a side of his dad that he had seen before. I didn't realize it was a scare tactic to keep me in check.

Small Town Drama

This was the first moment I'd witnessed Leo go off the rails. But it wouldn't be the last. I couldn't say much though because it didn't take much for Sarena to send me off the rails. And she was always there with something. One day, Leo's daughter called us up and said, "Dad, Sarena had to take the baby to the emergency room. How come you're not answering your phone? She wants you to get over there right now."

> Relationships are meant to have a third wheel.

There was no way I was going to let her pull his strings like that so I told him I was going with him. When we got to the hospital, she glared at me and said, "What's she doing here?"

He said, "Sarena, just mind your own business."

She told the security, "I don't want her to come back here with me."

I'm a nurse practitioner so of course they know me at the hospital. He looked at me and asked, "Ms. Harris, what's wrong?"

I said, "I want to go back there with my boyfriend and she is saying she doesn't want me back there." It's a small town, they knew me, so they let me go back. She started screaming and hollering that she didn't want me back there. Leo got so angry, he left me at the hospital so I had to call his sister to pick me up.

"What do you mean he left you at the hospital?" his sister asked, "Don't tell me you're at the hospital clowning with Sarena."

When I got to the house, he told me that we needed to talk because he couldn't live like this. He reassured me that he was with me and didn't understand why I couldn't get along with Sarena.

"No," I objected, "whenever she says jump, you go. That doesn't show me you're with me."

"But the baby was sick."

"There was nothing wrong with that baby. Are you gonna go up there every time he has a cold?"

We cooled down and then made up, physically. That was always the way things went, everything could be solved in bed. It didn't matter how angry he made me, because he'd always come home to me. I thought he loved me when in reality he simply knew how to keep me at bay. Things got so bad between me and Sarena that my mother called up Sarena's mother. She said, "I don't like the way these girls are behaving over Leo."

Her mother replied, "My daughter can handle herself; she'll be just fine."

My mother objected, "Well, I don't want my daughter caught up like this so shouldn't you talk to your daughter and I'll talk to my daughter?"

Her mother replied, "Leo and Sarena were together before your daughter broke them up. If she wants to stay with Leo, she can handle herself."

Just Checking In

In August, my mother had apparently heard more than she cared to hear and decided it was time to see for herself what was happening. I had been telling my sister Angie about all the drama Sarena was causing with her baby. On top of that, Leo's sister Shirley had also been calling my mom to let her know about everything that was happening. (I told you she orchestrated most of the drama.)

So, my parents, two of my aunts, their husbands, and some cousins came down for a visit. I went into "everything's fine" mode. I'm going to work, Leo is working, all is good. Up to this point, I hadn't realized the cleanliness of my house had been going downhill. When my mother asked why everything was so junky, I immediately went on the defense, "Maybe because I'm pregnant and tired."

I was oblivious that my environment was not matching what was happening emotionally in my life, things were chaotic to say the least. She told me that we needed to get the house ready for the baby and began cleaning things up for me.

I didn't even realize that my environment was a product of how things were going in my life. I kept a very clean house but I had stuff piled up everywhere. My mom said "we need to get this house ready for you to have a baby." My godmother, who lived in Louisiana, came up to help. Although I'm pretty sure now that she was only there to help my mother size Leo up. They wanted to know if he really was this cheater everyone said he was.

While she was there, my Aunt Annie told me that Leo pulled a gun on her. I dismissed what she was actually saying because Leo worked at the jail, he carried his gun like he carried his wallet.

Chapter 7

Mrs. Leonard & The Memphis Run

Shortly after my family left, Hurricane Katrina hit. I lost power and water so we went to stay at a hotel in West Helena, Arkansas. All the hotels in our areas were already flooded with people who had evacuated the coast. I was around nine months pregnant and he jumps up and says, "Let's get married."

I had been wanting to get married since he had proposed. In Arkansas, you didn't have to wait three days like Mississippi, you could just get hitched on the spot so we did. I wore capri pants and a t-shirt and he had on sunglasses the entire time. He held two of my fingers as he said his vows. It was like, *I'm only doing this because you want this.* There was no love in it but you couldn't have convinced me of that. This was the ultimate one-up on Sarena as far as I was concerned. They had been together five or six years and never gotten married. We got back to the house and I called up his sister, Carla, to tell her the news.

The phone started ringing off the hook, everyone was excited. Then, here comes good ol' Shirley, "I heard you all did it, girl. Sarena is crying her eyes out."

Sarena got so angry she filed a restraining order against me. I countered one on her for harassment. We took it all the way to court. The judge wasn't a stupid man. He looked at us and said, "This room is so full of tension right now I could cut it with a knife. Ladies, you are carrying his child and this one has his child. You two better figure out how to get along."

I said, "Your honor, I'm never going to get along with her."

He dismissed us out of court.

Baby Boy

They kept messing with my due date because they said I was measuring large and finally they had me do a c-section on October 5th. When my doctor examined me, she saw my pelvic bone hadn't widened and said, "You're just going to stay pregnant forever." I went in and had my beautiful boy. Leo was so delighted to name him Lenny Dean Smith III. I'm convinced that is the real reason he married me, because he wanted that III. He already had three sons named after him—Leonardo, Leonard, and Leo—but none of them carried his full name until now. Not a single one of his children, except my son, carried his last name because he either never married their mother or got married after they were born.

My mom and oldest sister flew down to take care of me and the baby. I had a big enough house for everyone to stay in but my sister insisted on staying at a hotel. It wasn't until years later that she confessed to feeling an evil presence in the house. That had been the reason she wouldn't stay. Everything seemed to finally be at peace.

When the baby was six weeks old, Leo and I went up to the church convention in Tennessee. I was excited to show the baby off and my parents were happy we were finally married. For once Shirley wasn't stirring up any trouble, from October to April, everything was good. Or so I thought.

With Friends Like That Who Needs Enemies

One day, I received a call from a pharmacist telling me he had a prescription from me but it didn't look like my handwriting. I asked him to send me copies of all the prescriptions he had filled that had been requested by me. As I looked through all the names I grew concerned because none of these names looked familiar, then I came across a familiar name. I called up my friend, Shirley, and asked what she had done.

She started crying, "I'm sorry. I'm addicted." She had stolen my prescription pad back in October and had been writing prescriptions under my name and license. I didn't want to go to prison so I told Leo what had happened and surrendered my license to the state of Mississippi. I closed down my practice and got a Tennessee nursing license. I started working in Memphis so I would have to leave the house at 7:00 just to get to work by 8:30. I told Leo this would be the perfect time for us to move and start fresh.

He, however, became convinced that I wanted to move to Memphis because I had a man in Memphis. One morning I woke up and my brand-new truck wouldn't start. When I told him, he said, "You're not going anywhere today. I unplugged your battery. I had somebody follow you and I know you're going up there to see a man."

"You mean the male nurses I work with?" I laughed, "I'm not seeing no man."

I called my sister Angie and told her what was going on. She called the police and because the town is so small the police told her, "We're gonna send somebody over there to tell Leo to stop acting like that."

Unfamiliar with the small town, everybody-knows-everybody atmosphere, she said, "Tell him to stop? My sister has got to go to work!"

> A level-headed person would have left; they would have said, You're sick! You need help." But I stayed. Why did I stay with this fool?

Thanks to Angie's quick thinking I got to work that day.

There was a full-blown investigation once I turned in the evidence surrounding my prescription pad. During which they discovered she was part of a larger drug ring. She was giving all the drugs to a dealer on the east coast. It took me thousands of dollars in attorney fees but I never spent a day behind bars and kept my name clean, thank God for great parents.

I told Leo maybe this was our chance to start fresh. I sold my house in three days and my mother flew down to help me pack and move. She had to because Leo wanted nothing to do with the move and neither did his family. When the check was sent for the sale of the house, Leo cashed it and didn't tell me he had the money. I told him we needed to move because we couldn't live off of his income alone and I could no longer practice in Mississippi. When I asked his father if the family could help me load the truck he refused because I was trying to take his son away. I couldn't understand any of this, it was only an hour away.

My dad knew a pastor in Memphis and one of his church members was a realtor. She found me a beautiful three bedroom on a hill to rent. From everything with the prescription pad theft, having to transfer my license, having a new baby, getting a new job, and the move—I was frazzled. I told Leo I didn't want any of his kids coming to stay with us for a while. We needed time to ourselves with the baby.

Here Comes Crazy

My Aunt Barbara Jean and my mother came to help me unpack everything and get settled into the house. The night they arrived we went out to get new keys made. When we got back to the house Leo was sitting in the living room. He stared at me coldly and said, "You thought you could lock me out?"

I said, "What are you talking about? I have a key right here for you."

Come to find out, he had broken the kitchen window and had his daughter climb through to unlock the door. Looking back, I suppose he was trying to establish his dominance in the relationship. I had told him not to bring any kids and here his daughter and niece were with him. No respect for me at all. Whatever spell he had on me was now gone because I looked at this fool and told him he either needed to take the girls home or get them a hotel room but they were not staying at the house with us. I was fed up with drama.

The Prayer Room

I didn't think too much about him breaking into the house but my mother and Aunt Barbara Jean saw it for what it was-absolute bananas! No sane person does something like that. Recently my Aunt told me that my mom had tried to get Leo to go with her to the Prayer Room at the Church of God in Christ in Memphis. She thought if she could get him there then maybe he would change. But it was at this moment when they decided I needed to get away from Leo so that is what they began to pray for.

Chapter 8

Downhill to Destruction

There were so many flags in my first marriage to Mark, the night of our wedding being the first. And it was no different with Leo. Yet, I continued to stay despite all the craziness and despite all the signs, I continued to stay. Friends and family members were picking up on stuff; some tried to warn me and others thought it best to mind their business. Either way, I wish I wouldn't have been so desperate to have someone in my life that I ignored everything in front of me.

Leo never moved to Memphis. He'd come up and stay a couple nights with me and Lenny but the rest of the time he stayed at his two-bedroom shack next to his parent's house. The same place he was living when we were dating. He always said it was too much of a drive for him to get to work. Funny that it never seemed to matter when I had to drive an hour every day to work in Memphis. I kept telling him to transfer but he wouldn't.

When you're the only one making sacrifices, don't believe the lie that you're the selfish one. Because it will attack you if you let it!

My mom flew back home after a month. She made sure to help me get everything lined up for Lenny since Leo wasn't helping in any way. She saw that Monday-Friday I was on my own, basically a single parent making sure everything was taken care of with the baby. It wasn't easy. We'd go stay with him in the shack for a few nights here and there. I did this mainly to reassure myself that I still had a husband. We went on for nine months until his visits started becoming fewer. He wouldn't come up for two or three weeks and I began feeling like I was losing him. I knew I'd have to return to Mississippi if I wanted to keep my husband. There was no way he was going to move or change jobs. I broke my lease in the fall of 2006 and moved back to Clarksdale. This time his father was happy to help me move.

I moved back and moved into his little shack of a house. The reason he said move back was because he said his father was going to give us a half an acre to build a house. He had convinced me that he was going to build me a beautiful brick home, French doors, sunken living room, and it was going to be gorgeous. I went back and we were in the little shack.

I had moved to Memphis like February or March. This is now 2006. I moved back that fall like November. This is when all kinds of hell is getting ready to break loose.

Backsliding to The Backwoods

As I mentioned at the beginning of the book, I grew up in a very privileged home. We had nice stuff and we took care of our nice stuff. There was always a sense of pride with our accomplishments. Not everyone lives in that same kind of mindset. Leo was perfectly content with living in his tin-roof shack out in the boondocks. When I left Memphis and moved into Leo's house there were some people I didn't even tell because deep down I was ashamed of my living conditions. However, I had worked so hard to get Leo that it seemed like a waste to lose him now. I had to move back with my husband.

Another element of moving back was that Leo didn't want me to work in Memphis anymore. To some extent, living and working in Memphis allowed me to have some independence and I think he realized that took away some of his control over me. I got a job at the local high school teaching Anatomy. When my parents came down for one of their yearly visits, I did my best to paint a beautiful picture. This God forsaken shack in the middle of nowhere wasn't that bad, it was only our transition home because Leo was going to build us a home. It was all going to be good. My father was very quiet during their visit. Years later I found out that he had called my sister crying asking, "Why would Jackie live like that?"

I was truly blinded by what I thought love was. The truth was that I wasn't happy, I was settling more and more each day. And each lie I told myself about how things would get better and how good we were doing only hurt me more. Each lie entrapped me further in this illusion because lies cannot bring freedom. Only speaking the truth, including to yourself, can truly free someone.

> "Then you will know the truth, and the truth will set you free." John 8:32

What's Done in The Dark

The rumors about Leo and Sarena continued to circulate around town. There was never a moment that they had died down but somehow, I had gotten to a point that I really didn't listen to them anymore. My girlfriend, Mary, called me up one day and asked, "What if I told you Leo is seeing Sarena, what would you do?"

I love Mary and have so much respect for her but her question caught me off guard. I said, "What would I do? I don't know what do you want me to do?"

She said, "Jackie, he's seeing her."

"No, they're not seeing each other like that. He goes over there to see the baby."

She said, "No, you're not listening to me. Do you hear what I'm saying to you? I am saying that he is ***SEEING*** her."

Hearing her say this brought on such a mixture of emotions. And confronting Leo never did any good. By the beginning of 2007, I was longing for Seattle. Maybe if I got back home, I could start over and things would be better. I finally worked up the courage to tell Leo I needed a break. I wanted to fly out to Seattle and take a break.

In that moment, he pulled a rifle on me and said, "You're not gonna leave me."

He chased me around the yard with the rifle. In my mind I tried to talk down the craziness of the situation like, *Oh he's just messing.* But in my heart, I knew he was crazy. Nobody chases someone around with a loaded gun just to mess with them. I was laughing to avoid showing I was scared. "What's wrong with you?"

"If you think you'll ever leave me; I'll kill you first."

I ran up to his parent's house and told his father, "Leo's out here chasing me with a gun."

His dad said, "Boy stop playing with that girl." Leo had a fit because I was talking crazy. His dad pulled me aside and asked what was going on. I told him things were really bad between us. He was staying out late and everyone was telling me he'd been out with Sarena.

I don't know what he said to Leo but he ended up telling me I could go stay with my sister for two weeks. I told him I was going to help my sister with her daycare so I could make some money while I was up there. But in my mind, I knew that I really didn't want to return to Mississippi.

While there was distance between us, I developed some nerves of steel. He'd call me day and night promising that things would be better when I came back home. While I was there, I asked why he never allowed me to see his cell phone. Then I told him that one time he was sleeping, I saw that Sarena had sent him a text and asked him what he was doing. Why was that?

I'm telling you, this distance made me bold.

He didn't appreciate my boldness. He told me the reason he didn't show me his phone was because it was his business. I explained that since we were married, I didn't think it should work that way but he replied that I should trust him and the conversation was dropped. Despite the desire to leave, I still loved Leo, or at least I thought I did, so I returned to Mississippi after the two weeks was up. My friend could not believe I came back. She told me I should have just stayed away. When I said I loved Leo she was adamant that what I had was not love, "Jackie, he has a whole other life. He's seeing another woman, don't you care?"

> Take note, only cheaters have something to hide. Healthy marriages don't have secrets, they are all about intimacy, making things known.

I cared enough to bring it up to Leo but he always told me they were lying or jealous of him. And I believed him, for whatever sorry reason, I believed him and I stayed; getting pulled further and further into the madness.

Catina's Stakeout

News was circulating around my family that I wasn't doing very well; even though I did my best to put on a good show. It got to my cousin Catina who was a few months older than me, my "twin" cousin. If you remember, she was the same cousin who wanted to warn me about Mark. Catina had recently gotten hurt and was going to be having surgery. So, she called me up and said she wanted to spend some time with me before her surgery.

We had always been close but the last thing I wanted her to see was me living in a shack. I was Jaqueline the nurse practitioner, the star of the family that went to college. I had this big old wedding, and the nice things, I couldn't let anybody see me failing. So, when she called to tell me she was at my house I didn't really take her seriously. Even though she had been talking about it for some time I acted like I had no idea she was coming. There was no way I could be excited about her coming to visit, if Leo saw me excited it would have been hell to pay. He was always fearful that if someone saw how I was living they would take me away. When she got to the house, it was raining; I had buckets scattered around the house to catch the rain coming in through the roof.

Leo looked up at her and asked, "Why are you here?"

"I'm just here to see Jackie."

I don't remember a whole lot about the visit but Catina told me I lit up a cigarette like I was really nervous. I think I was probably nervous about what Leo might say since he was never a fan of my family coming to town. Catina had a hotel room so I went with her to hang out at the hotel under the stipulation from Leo that I "better be back." We picked up my friend Laura and the three of us were hanging out together. Unbeknownst to me, Laura pulled Catina aside and told her that she was worried about me. Everybody in town knew that Leo was still seeing Sarena but I refused to accept it or leave.

Catina and Laura decided that night that they were going to do a stakeout on my behalf. They decided to sit in front of Sarena's house to see if they could get to the bottom of things. Sure enough, Leo showed up at the house, stayed for a few hours, and left around two in the morning. They even took pictures! When they presented their evidence to me, they thought for sure a smart woman like me would finally see things for what they were but instead I went ballistic. What they didn't realize is that Leo had already threatened me multiple times that he'd kill me if I left him. And while I was entirely sure he would hold true to his threats; the thought alone was enough to make me stay put.

"This is why I didn't even want you to come." I yelled, "How dare you come up in here and act like you know what's going on. I'm going back to my house with my man. You carry on with your life and you be on your way."

I knew that I had hurt her but I was in too deep to accept the truth. The truth didn't give me a way out, it only proved more complications. It was better for me to suck it up and carry on. Protect my man and love my man. Accepting the truth would only feel defeating.

On the way back to Texas, she called our aunt, "I just left Jackie's and she's not in a good place."

After going into all the details of everything she saw our aunt said, "Oh my god, we've got to get a plan to get Jackie out of Mississippi."

"I don't know what you guys are going to do. She's not going to leave him. I had pictures and she refused to accept that he was cheating."

My aunt lit up the grapevine. She called my sister Angie and my sister called my mother. They started a full-fledged prayer conference on the matter. My sister made up this "potion," I'm not really sure what else to call it. It was a mixture of anointing oil and dirt then sent it to me. She called me and said, "I want you to place that on the four corners of your house outside. I'm praying that every person plotting evil against you will turn away."

I figured they were praying Leo would stop clowning and Sarena would stop her drama. I had no idea they were praying me out of Mississippi.

Chapter 9

A Damaged Ego

Reflecting on everything that happened during my relationship with Leo now feels like someone watching the same episode on repeat. Every holiday, drama. Every family event, drama. And the name of every episode was Sarena. This woman was the bane of my existence. What I didn't know then but I can look back and see now, Sarena was never my enemy. My enemy was a bunch of spirits pulling all the strings. The drama and gossip that Shirley loved creating, the lust and selfishness that kept Leo doing what he wanted when he wanted. All too often we pick our battles with what we can see and forget that there is so much more going on under the surface.

> "For our struggle is not against flesh and blood, but against the rulers, against the authorities, against the powers of this dark world and against the spiritual forces of evil in the heavenly realms." Ephesians 6:12

Jealous Rage

As time went on, Leo's jealousy showed more and more. He began accusing me of cheating on him more and more. I suppose when someone has guilt gnawing inside of them it can have a way of convincing you everyone around you is guilty of the same thing. Lust was his vice so naturally he assumed it was mine too. There were numerous occasions where his jealousy showed its evil head. One of those times was at his sister's house.

Although I never knew him to be on drugs, there were sure times when he acted like he was out of his mind on something. This time, he sped up to his sister's house, hit the fence with the bumper of his car, and came pounding on the door. She threw open the door, "What's wrong with you?"

"I'm coming to find Jackie."

"What do you mean find her? She's right here."

"I know what's going on. You guys are helping her cheat on me."

His sister shook her head. "Man, you have really lost it."

He reached over his sister, grabbed me by my hair and pulled me out of the house onto the porch. I was screaming and hollering. I wasn't sure what he had planned for me, or even what he assumed I was doing. His sister was fighting him, hitting him, and screaming for him to leave me alone. I got free and we both ran into the house.

She slammed the door and said, "My brother has lost his mind."

"Yes, he has, because I'm not cheating on him."

She called up her parents and told them Leo was at her house and had lost his mind because he thought I was cheating on him. Did she call the police? No. Did anyone call the police? No. His parents would say, "Tell that boy to stop it." And that's how it was handled.

A Little Bit Stronger

The dichotomy between me and Sarena was different from jealous rage. I had my suspicions she was messing around with my husband, but I didn't want to believe it. I wanted to think the best of him and our marriage. But whenever she'd show her face my blood would boil. I believe she was in the same boat on her side. She had been with Leo for a while now and he was still pulling her strings. Giving her just enough to keep us both happy from one moment to one moment. But neither of us wanted to share the man and deep down we both knew we were, her more than me, of course. I was always in denial, a cheater for a husband wasn't something that would happen to me.

Father's Day 2007 comes around and by this time everyone has been trying to convince me Leo is cheating, family and friends. Which is why, when Sarena's golden SUV pulls up to the family cookout—it gets real! The year before I had walked away but this year, I'm openly livid about the matter. She is not welcome especially since everyone around town is already saying you're seeing each other. "Is she seriously coming up here?"

"Let's not start this today." His father said trying to keep the peace.

I ignored him and glared at Sarena, "Who invited you?"

"Your husband invited me."

Leo was standing by the grill cooking, "I didn't tell you to come here."

Leo's sisters were sitting there with their eyes wide waiting for World War III to bust out as we start screaming at each other. Thankfully Leo's mom had enough sense to settle things down, "Ya'll please stop this. Sarena, get a plate and go. Jackie is Leo's wife and you know the two of you don't get along. You need to leave."

Sarena got a plate and stormed off but for me that was the very last straw. Leo's sister Carla, was always very calm and diplomatic. She never started drama like Shirley. She looked at me and said, "Jackie, there's a reason you and her can't get along."

I said, "There sure is, Carla, because I get along with the rest of his children's mothers just fine."

Deep down, I knew they were hooking up. As much as I wanted to ignore it, I knew it was true but I didn't know how to properly leave. This time, I called my sister and said, "Send me a plane ticket, I'm leaving Leo."

"What happened?"

"Sarena and I got into it."

And with that I packed a suitcase for myself and the baby, drove up to my friend's house in Memphis, and flew out to Seattle. Leo was blowing up my phone but I didn't answer until I arrived at the airport. "Leo, I'm in Seattle. I left you because I'm tired of you and Sarena."

"You left me?" It was the first time I'd heard shook in his voice, "And you took my baby?"

"Yes, I did and I'm really done."

"Where's your truck?"

"It's none of your business where it is."

He gave me the same ol' song and dance he always sung. He wasn't cheating, everyone was making stuff up, he wanted me back. I took a few weeks to cool down and clear my head then went back to Mississippi. I know what you're thinking, she went back again!? Yes, because like I said, I didn't know how to leave properly. It wasn't just about getting some distance, there were heart strings that needed to be cut. As long as those stayed connected, Leo could always find a way to pull me back like his puppet on a string.

The Other Man

Although I didn't know how to leave, when I returned to Mississippi, I decided to give him an ultimatum. It was time for things to change or I would be leaving. At the same time, child support papers showed up in the mail. The only thing worse than a cheater is a cheater with a damaged ego. Leo looked at the papers and was furious, "I know she didn't."

Shirley had told me at work that Sarena had got another man because she didn't want Leo anymore. I thought it was just Shirley trying to stir up more drama but when I saw the papers I began to wonder if it was true. That's the only reason I could see her filing for child support.

He called her up and started arguing with her, things got heated, and then he stormed out of the house. He didn't get back home until two in the morning. When I asked where he had gone, he said he just needed time to cool down. When I had given him the ultimatum, he had assured me that I wasn't going to leave him because he was going to do better. And for a while everything was going good. Then they started to get weird.

He'd wake up and his tires would be slashed or he'd be driving down the road and his tire would fall. He was convinced that someone was after him. I had no idea who would be angry enough with him to do that kind of stuff. Come to find out, they thought it might be Sarena's boyfriend causing all the problems.

You're Gonna Die

Things never settled between me and Sarena. We were always on edge in each other's presence. Then one day, as I was driving into choir rehearsal Leo called me. Someone had loosened his bolts again and he was stuck on the side of the road. I pulled up to his car at the same time Sarena pulled up with Leo's uncle. Seeing her there threw me into a frenzy.

> "Hearts made of stone don't bend, they crack when pushed too far." -H. M. Ward

I jumped out of my car with a box cutter ready to slice her neck. But she was just as crazy as I was because she jumped out of her car and ran towards me. I yelled, "That's it, today you're gonna die!"

Leo grabbed me and his uncle grabbed Sarena. We're hollering and cussing; I'm calling her all kinds of names. (None of them are nice ones.) We're just going back and forth. Leo's holding me back and screaming for him to let me go.

"What's wrong with you?"

"What do you mean, what's wrong with me? Your ex-woman is here acting like she's going to rescue you." He told me to go home and cool down. "I can't, I've got choir rehearsal."

I went to the church and I was livid. The pastor told me to come into his office to talk for a moment. I unloaded everything; I mean everything. And he said, "Well, that's your husband. Things are gonna get better, don't worry. God is gonna see you through."

I'm crying. This time, my pastor has convinced me to stay.

Burn It All

I'm pretty sure the last thing God wanted me to do was stay with this man. It's one thing to work through those tough times in a marriage but at this point, everything was lining up for me to cut my losses and get away. I woke up one morning to smoke coming out from behind the fridge. I got the baby, ran over to Leo's parent's house, and told his dad something was wrong with the fridge. When we got back to the shack it was on fire. His dad grabbed a water hose and was trying to put the fire out. We were way out in the country so by the time the fire department got to us the whole house was on fire.

The house was unlivable. The fire inspector determined the house caught fire due to improper wiring. When the insurance company asked who had done the wiring and Leo said he was the one who had done it, they didn't want to pay. Red Cross put us up in a hotel for two weeks. During our stay at the hotel, Leo really starts showing his true colors. I barely see him during the stay and every time I question where he's been he has an excuse. I'm not sure if he had reached a point where he was too confident in his control over me or what was happening but things were certainly slipping.

Chapter 10

Welcome to the Circus

In January 2008, Leo seemed to be slipping off what little rails he had. His sister Shirley was throwing a birthday party for herself, as she usually did, and Sarena showed up to the party. I had already prepared myself to act civil because it was Shirley's house and Sarena was her friend. Leo jumped up and asked for my keys the moment she walked in.

"Where are you going?"

"I'm not gonna stay here because y'all are gonna fight."

I refused to give him my keys because I knew I wasn't going to start something. He stormed out of Shirley's house and about that same time I noticed Sarena leave as well. By the time he comes back to the house I'm in my vehicle getting ready to leave. He gets into the truck and I started punching him in the face. We started an all-out fist fight in the car, in her driveway. A neighbor called the police and the officer who responded ended up being someone he went to school with.

When he asked what was going on Leo said, "Oh nothing, we cool, we cool."

I had my face turned so the officer couldn't see me crying. He asked if I was ok and I lied. I'm not sure how things went down in big cities but, I knew there would be no help from this man who was his friend whether he was an officer or not. Leo was 6'4, he had huge hands. It would have been clear to anyone who walked up to the vehicle that night; things were not ok. But when everybody is everybody's friend, you turn a blind eye because "we cool."

By this time, our house had been repaired but I didn't want to go home. I called Leo's dad and asked if I could stay at their house. I took the baby and stayed with them. When his dad saw me, he was really upset. He stood on the back porch and yelled at Leo, "What have you done to this girl?"

"Dad, just leave it alone."

I woke up the next morning and acted like nothing happened. When you're experiencing that kind of trauma everything kicks into survival mode. You just start going through motions to stay alive while no longer living. You don't have an opinion, an agenda, a dream, or a drive, at that point you wake up every day just hoping to survive.

The next day he was apologizing and promising me he'd never hit me again. I was crying. I wanted to believe him but it just didn't feel like love. Up to this point, my will hadn't been broken. I still felt comfortable threatening to leave him. It was the game I played in hopes that he would turn things around.

But when you play with fire it doesn't take long before you get burned.

I Ain't Playing

I noticed Sarena's number on Leo's phone like she had tried calling him back-to-back. This of course initiated an argument and I once again resorted to getting away. Maybe that would show him he didn't deserve me. Maybe he'd finally come to his senses and stop fooling with Sarena. Little did I know, this would be the day Leo would be done. I jumped in my truck with the baby in the backseat. He opened the door, pulled me from the truck and said, "That's it you're not leaving me anymore."

He pulled out his 9mm, put me in the car, got in the driver's seat, and drove me out to this dark country road. He parked the car and pointed the gun at me, "Before you leave me again, I'll kill you. The next time your parents come to get you they will come get you in a body bag."

"Jesus, Jesus, Jesus." Was the only thing I could manage to say at first, then I begged, "Don't kill me in front of our child."

"Then tell me you won't leave me!" He demanded waving the gun in my face.

"Just put the gun down, I won't leave you."

"Do you promise?"

"I promise! Just put the gun down."

"Pay attention to this road." He waved the gun around, "Because nobody will find you out here."

I promised not to leave him once more and we went back home.

Exit Stage Left

Even though I had promised, I knew it was time to leave for real, no more games. If he caught me leaving, he'd kill me but if I stayed, he might also kill me. The school year ended in May, if I could just hold out until then I'd get three months pay and could start over in Seattle. I wanted to be sure I had some money to start over.

Leo's coming and going as he pleases, staying out all night. We're still fighting but trying to ride things out so I can get to summer. Then one particular morning in March, Leo walks in with two plates of breakfast food. I'll never forget, it was bacon, eggs, and two pieces of toast. When I asked him where he had got the food, he told me not to worry about it. I just stared at him in disbelief. He had obviously brought it from somebody's house but he was going to play it off like it was no big deal?

In April, he was fired. It wasn't his fault, oh no, it's always someone else's fault. The worst part was that he didn't tell me he was fired. I was sitting there, at his job, waiting to pick him up. He wasn't answering his phone and then I found out he wasn't even there. I ended up leaving. This was now normal behavior.

"I'll answer my phone if I feel like it. If I don't, then I don't."

"I don't have to come home at night, I'm a grown man."

He had zero respect for me and zero responsibility. He was going to do what he wanted, when he wanted to do it, and nobody was going to tell him otherwise. I'm not sure why I ever accepted this as ok. My father would NEVER treat my mother that way. April 2008 was probably the worst month of our entire marriage. The fighting during that month was just awful.

And to make matters worse, I still have people coming to me, telling me that he is involved with Sarena. One of his cousins subtly asked me one day, "Do you know where your husband is?"

"Where do you think he is?"

He looked at me in shock, "You don't know where he is?"

"Where do you think he is?" I asked again.

He shook his head. "All I'm gonna say is you need to find Sarena and you'll find your husband."

He lost another job the second week of April. I couldn't understand it, one minute they were bragging on him and the next they let him go. Leo brushed it off like it was no big deal. He'd find another job but in the meantime him and his uncle would start fixing up the house. April was when everything changed. We started this routine. He'd drop the baby off at day-care, then drop me off at work before going back to the house and doing whatever it was he was doing. But during that time, he began drinking heavily and became non-respondent. He'd always been into me but not anymore.

The Duffle Bag

In the third week of April, I noticed a duffle bag in the car—brown khakis and a white t-shirt. I asked him what the duffle bag was for and he told me not to worry about it. Typically, that would throw me into defense mode, I'm not a stupid woman. But that day I wasn't even in the mood to start something. He dropped off the baby at daycare, dropped me off at work, and I went about my day.

But when he picked me up from work, he was no longer wearing his red shorts and green t-shirt; now he was wearing the clothes from the duffle bag. Now, I could no longer keep my mouth shut. "Why'd you have to change clothes?"

"My clothes got really dirty from working on the house and I didn't want to come pick you up all messy and dirty."

We left the school and went to his friend's house to watch the basketball game. The baby didn't have to be picked up from daycare until six. We'd usually have a few beers with his friend to unwind before picking him up. On the way to his friend's house, I asked how his day went.

He got a huge smile on his face and said, "We gonna be alright. We not gonna have no more problems."

"What do you mean?"

He glanced at me. "I want to apologize to you for how I've been treating you and everything that's been going down with Sarena."

I wasn't sure what he was planning but I wasn't about to be played. I had the eeriest feeling. "What have you done? Or what are you trying to do?"

"Nothing babe, nothing. I'm just letting you know from now on we're not going to fight no more, I'm not going to pull pistols on you no more, we are gonna be solid."

He'd treated me downright awful for the past year. I'd been hit, threatened, and disrespected. I wasn't even sure who this man in the car with me was. He pulled up to his friend's place, gave me a kiss, and we went inside.

Chapter 11

Where's Sarena?

Ten minutes after we get to his friend's place, Shirley calls me, "Hey, Jackie, I don't mean to call you with no confusion but Sarena and her baby are missing. Her mother is looking for them. Can you ask Leo if he has seen them?"

Leo rolled his eyes, "I don't know why she's asking me. I don't know. She's a grown woman, she can go where she wants."

His phone started ringing like crazy and he said, "Mom and dad said we need to get back to the house quickly."

We picked up the baby from daycare and headed home. Normally, he'd take the short cut through the field but today he took the long way home. When we pulled up to the house his parents and uncle were getting out of their truck. They had just come home from fishing. He pulled his uncle to the side and started talking to him. I wasn't sure what they were talking about but I didn't have a good feeling.

A few minutes later, Sarena's sister pulled up to the house with Sarena's daughter and parents. She jumped out of the car and said, "Where's my sister?"

Leo brushes them off telling them he has no idea but she is insistent. I'm wondering why they think my husband would know where Sarena is but they weren't stupid. They all knew Leo and Sarena had been sneaking around for the past few years, and they all knew Sarena was finally trying to move on. One of his sisters called him and told him the police were heading to the house to question him. My hands began to tremble; I couldn't stop shaking. Why were they coming to question him?

He told me to get in the car but I couldn't understand why we'd leave. He didn't know where she was. We went back to his friend's house and then the police showed up. Leo handed me his gold bracelets, rings, watch, and wallet then told me to take all of it home.

"Why are you giving me all this? They're just here to ask you questions."

The officers looked at me and said they needed me to come down to the station for questioning as well. They were taking Leo down in the police car but told me I'd be ok to follow them down. I couldn't believe they seriously thought we had something to do with Sarena being missing. I asked his friend's girlfriend to watch the baby and followed them to the police station.

They took us into separate rooms and started asking me if I knew anything about Sarena and her baby missing. I was annoyed. This woman had been a thorn in my side since day one. "Sir, I was at work and I don't have anything further to say to you. If you have anything else to say to me you can speak to my attorney."

The officer raised his eyebrows. "Why do you need an attorney?"

"Because something about this doesn't seem right."

"So, I can't record your statement?"

"No, I don't have anything to say to you. I was at work, if you have anything else to say to me you can call my attorney."

I passed Leo as I was walking to the lobby and he asked me if I could bring him some food. All his sisters were in the lobby looking like the cat had just swallowed the canary. One of them said, "I hope Sarena's not tied up in a house beat up."

I looked at her with confusion. "By who?"

She sighed. "Well sometimes my brother loses his cool."

I couldn't believe they even thought Leo might be involved. Everybody left the police station and said they were going to look for Sarena. I went to pick up the baby and called my sister. I was beginning to get freaked out. Sarena and her baby were missing, Leo had been arrested because they suspected he had something to do with it. My sister calmed me down a little, "She's probably just with her dude and doesn't want anybody to know where she is, she's grown."

Could It Be?

All this went down on Wednesday. My phone was ringing off the hook asking me if I've heard from Sarena. They had questioned Sarena's daughter's dad, they questioned Leo, and two other guys. At this point, everyone had been released except for Leo. I wasn't sure what to think.

By Thursday morning, I was emotional and mentally drained. I called my boss to let her know I wouldn't be able to teach and what was happening.

She said, "Even if you were ok to come in, I couldn't let you. It's circulating all over town that Sarena and her baby are missing and your husband has been arrested. Take off and handle whatever it is you've got to do."

I wasn't even sure what to think when I hung up the phone. This was not what I had planned for my life. I couldn't believe that my husband had been arrested because his ex-girlfriend and child were missing. On the way to drop the baby off at daycare, I passed by the search and rescue scene. I walked up to some of Leo's family and asked if Sarena was still missing. They told me she was but her car had been found and there was blood in the trunk.

"Hey, Jackie, come here." Leo's uncle waved me away from the others, "The other day when Leo took me by the shed to talk. He said if anybody asks where I have been you need to tell them I was with you all day." He looked around then looked back at me. "But I wasn't with him. I was with his mom and dad fishing. Why would he tell me that? I don't wanna get involved with this stuff."

At that moment, I remember asking Leo about a gash on his leg when he picked me up from work. He had said he'd got it from working on the house but now that his uncle was telling me this, I was beginning to connect the pieces. He had changed his clothes; he'd told me we were gonna be alright. Could he have done something to her?

Bad Blood Boiling

Just then, Sarena's mother ran towards me hollering, "Why is she here?"

I said, "Let's do this, I'm here to help find Sarena."

Sarena's mother had made it clear that she thought I stole Leo from her daughter. The sheriff walked up and told me I couldn't be at the search site. I didn't understand what the issue was. Regardless of our past history, Sarena was a human being. She had a child and her child was my child's sibling. I just wanted to help find her. And it was in that moment when I dropped to my knees and lost it crying. This woman and her baby were missing and they wouldn't let me help because my husband was a suspect. On top of that, people are looking at me like I'm a suspect too.

Leo's daughter was there and offered to take the baby to daycare for me. She took the baby and I went to my friend's house. I told her I needed to stay with her for a little while and she said, "Yeah you do, things are getting bad."

I wasn't there too long before the phone rang. I was summoned back to Leo's parent's house for a family meeting. They had decided Leo was going to need an attorney. There's blood in the car, they can't find Sarena or the baby, and he's their only suspect. It's not looking good. Then Avery calls crying, "They found my brother, they found him in a field tied up, he's got to go to the hospital but he's alive."

Suddenly I found myself back at the police station for questioning. They've heard that Sarena and I have a history of fighting. Once again, I'm back in the hot seat. "Yes, I don't like Sarena but neither does his ex-wife, Jessica. But like I said I don't know why you're questioning me. I was at work."

One of the officers said maybe I could ask my husband if he knew anything but another officer stopped me because he said anything I found out wouldn't hold up in court. Then they informed me that Leo and Sarena had met that morning for breakfast at Burger King.

"What!?" I knew I wasn't crazy. For all the times he tried to convince me they had broken things off, I knew at that moment that my suspicions had been correct. They'd never really called things off; they had only taken breaks. The homemade breakfast he had brought home, all the nights he'd stayed out late, every person trying to convince me they were hooking up.

When I got out of the police station I went home and everybody was at his parent's house once again. They asked me if I was going to pay for Leo's attorney.

"Oh no I'm not! That fool was with Sarena the day she disappeared."

They called up the top defense attorney in Mississippi and were trying to figure out how they were going to come up with the money for his retainer fee. It was something like five to ten thousand. I was just shaking my head, there was no way I was spending a dime to help that lying cheater. He'd made this mess for himself and he could figure his own way out of it.

Chapter 12

The Monster & The Kidnapping

They called the top Mississippi defense attorney, Johnny Wall. He said something like he needed a five or ten thousand retainer to take the case. We're all talking about how much it is going to cost, I'm still saying I ain't paying, when the phone rings. "We found Sarena." Everybody let out a sigh of relief. But then they informed us that she was dead. The room went into an emotional uproar. His sister cried out, "But she has babies, why would somebody do that?"

His mother was devastated, "They've got my baby, for this?"

Everybody left, I took the baby to our house but the night wasn't over. Cars keep passing by the house and turning off their lights like they were trying to intimidate me. I had to have police surveillance for me and my child. Word about how gruesome the crime scene was going around town. Then there were rumors that she was pregnant and it was going to be charged as a capital murder. They said Sarena's three-year-old was an eye-witness in the case. He had finally told investigators, "Daddy hurt mama."

Leo's daughter Avery, also attended the school I worked at. She called me up, "Mama Jackie, everybody keeps saying that you had something to do with this but I know you didn't because you were at work. I know you didn't do it. I saw you at work."

I reassured her. "You know I didn't, A."

I was distraught and confused. I didn't know what to do. The place where they found Sarena was the same place Leo had driven me and threatened to kill me. It was the same place he drove by on the way home when he took the long way the day Sarena went missing. I was absolutely sick. She was the mother of his child and he killed her. Not only that but he had left his son out there in the cold. He'd been bitten by bugs and animals; he'd even suffered dehydration. That could have been me and my baby! He could have done it to us.

The Monster

The friend we had visited the day Sarena went missing had a daughter who had gone to high school with Leo. She called me up after Sarena had been found and said, "I need to tell you about the monster that you're married to."

I said, "The monster?"

She said, "Yeah I need to tell you about the monster. Leo has had violent run-ins with ex-girlfriends since high school. This one girl he dated came to school with her hand burned. She said it was from cooking fried chicken but the truth was that Leo had dipped her hand in hot grease. And there was another girl he had tied up in the woods."

Despite all this, I was still in a confused state of denial. I could accept that he had been cheating on me with Sarena, but I couldn't bring myself to believe he had murdered her. If he was capable of that he could have been capable of anything which put so much more weight on every altercation we ever had.

Back in Seattle

By now, my family has learned about Sarena's murder and my sister Angie tells everyone, "It's time to get Jackie out of Mississippi." Angie was convinced that if Leo was going down for murder there was a good chance, he would somehow try to cover for himself. It is what I always did for him in the past.

> Domestic violence victims can only start over with a strong support system. Without this they will always stay.

My mother was very emotional to where she developed a spasm in her neck while my father was still hoping for the best. He tried to keep them calm by reminding them that I had a plan to finish out the school year and come up during summer break. Everyone seemed to settle down a bit until a family friend who had been to prison intervened and said, "You need to get her out of there now or he's going to drag her down with him."

In that very moment, Operation Evacuate Jackie from Mississippi was a go!

Aunt Flo decided she would be the one to do it. She said, "I'm going to act like I'm visiting family in West Memphis and then I'll just kidnap her and baby Lenny. Angie, you need to get her ready without spooking her though."

They knew I might not go willingly if I knew their plan. And they were probably right. I knew that something was up because my uncle called me and asked if I was ok. Then he said, "If someone is there to get you, don't resist, ok, Jackie?"

I wasn't quite sure what he meant but I said, "Ok."

Not long after, Angie called me and said, "Hey, Aunt Flo, is coming down and she wants to take you up to see family in West Memphis. Pack a bag for you and the baby."

I wasn't really in any state of mind to argue or really think about it so I said "ok" and went through the motions I needed to go through to fulfill her request.

Day 4

Sarena went missing on Wednesday. They found the baby on Thursday, then Sarena on Friday, and now we're at church on Sunday. There wasn't much time to think about anything. Every detail was all too raw and the emotions were too much. Sarena's son had been found behind the church. So, the pastor decided instead of having a service we were going to pray. All kinds of people showed up at this little bitty church. People who had never been there in their life just to see what they can see and hear what they can hear. Even the media was there.

I collapsed to the floor hollering and crying. One of my ex-coworkers, a male nurse, helped pick me up off the floor. Leo's dad said, "If you don't stop crying like this, they are going to think Leo is guilty."

I had no idea what to think. The baby was found and Sarena was dead. How should I be reacting? His family was way too calm and collected in my opinion. They had gotten a lawyer and kept saying everything was going to be ok. After the service, one of Leo's sons told me he wanted to talk. He said, "Mama Jackie, I don't think my dad did it."

I said, "Ok."

Then he went on to say, "Well, that's what we gonna say. People thought you had something to do with it but I told them you were at work so it couldn't have been you."

Once again that eerie feeling rose in my stomach. Were they trying to cover something up?

Nothing to See Here

Around 7PM on Sunday, Aunt Flo called to say she was on her way to pick me up. She was going to take me away to West Memphis for a few days to get away from all the crazy. She had already prepped her husband's family to let her do the talking. Her brother-in-law, his wife, and their son were all in the car. When she arrived, Leo's dad walked out, "How's it going, Aunt Flo?"

"Good." She smiled and waved at him, "We're going to take Jackie and the baby to visit for a few days."

He said, "Why don't you just leave the baby here?"

She waved her hand, "Oh no, they want to see the baby too."

I didn't have a clue what was about to happen or that Aunt Flo had a 38 pistol in her back pocket! Aunt Flo drove my car with me and the baby and we all headed to Arkansas. Somewhere along the way I started screaming and crying. My phone kept ringing and I was convinced that the police were coming to get me. They got to the hotel and checked in. Her sister-in-law had to sleep in the bed with me because I was so nervous. I didn't want to eat, get dressed, or wash my body. I couldn't function. Aunt Flo finally got me to lay down and rest.

I really don't remember a whole lot of what happened because I'm pretty sure I blocked it out because of the trauma. But when I woke up the next morning, and my aunt wasn't in the room, I called her screaming and crying. They had gone down to Walmart to pick up a few things. When they got back, I was so hysterical that she decided she needed to take me to the hospital. When we walked up to the nurse's desk I was screaming and crying, "Why did he kill her? He didn't have to kill her."

They took me in the back and gave me a shot to calm me down. My body was revolting against me from the lack of food and sleep I'd had over the past few days. I was a nervous wreck. They gave me an IV to rehydrate me and then sent me on my way with a prescription to calm me down. Aunt Flo called up Angie, "I can't put Jackie on a plane like this."

I don't know what Angie said but she got me on the plane. I don't even remember getting on to the plane. Since the tickets had been purchased last minute, our seats weren't next to each other. Aunt Flo acted a fool with the flight attendant's and said, "If you don't sit her by me this is not going to be a nice flight."

My parents were in Hawaii on their anniversary cruise so Angie and our god sister Felecia met Aunt Flo at the airport. Still to this day, I don't remember many details about how I actually got back to Seattle but thank God I had a family who loved me enough to kidnap and drug me for my own good! They managed to get me to my Aunt's house and my cousin had to carry me up the stairs. I kept saying I needed to call Leo. Angie convinced them to let me call but the jail wouldn't allow me to speak with him.

I don't know how things would have gone if it hadn't been for Angie. I left everything in Mississippi because I had no idea I was leaving for good. But she already had everything we would need in place—a place to stay, clothes, clothes for the baby, and furniture. Most people in domestic abuse situations have lots of excuses as to why they can't leave. I don't have a place, they had that covered. I don't have clothes, they had that covered. I don't have a job, Angie said, "You aren't working, you need to see a doctor."

My family was there to support me every step of the way as I began my climb back from nothing. I had to trust my family to have my back. Even though everyone in Seattle believes Leo is capable and guilty, I still have my doubts. I had a baby with him. I could not believe that he was so evil he would do that to his child and his mother. He left that baby tied up in the woods, crying all night in the rain while bugs, snakes, and animals bite him. I just couldn't believe that I was married to a person that was capable of that.

I see the doctor. He confirms I have had a nervous breakdown and I'm also suffering from situational anxiety disorder. He prescribes me an antidepressant and something to help me sleep. I refused the anti-depressants but took the sleeper at night so I could rest. Then in May, I began therapy with an amazing therapist. She was an African-American woman and she was phenomenal. As I tell her about everything that I have gone through in my marriage to Leo, she informs me that Leo is a sociopath. As different things started lining into place and I began acknowledging the behaviors I saw, I started to realize that Leo really must have done this.

I saw her every week for an entire year before it dropped down to once a month for six months.

Chapter 13

Moving On

Leo began calling me collect from the jail. He continued to tell me he didn't do it. "Why would I do that to Sarena? Somebody set me up."

In November, they subpoenaed me for the trial but my therapist provided a letter to excuse me stating it would be too traumatic for me to experience court. My girlfriend Laura went to all the trials and gave me blow by blow. She said, "Jackie, when Jessica gave her testimony of him taking a cord and choking her; she done put the nail in his coffin."

After hearing about this, I called his ex-wife and asked her why she'd never warned me. She simply said that I wouldn't have believed her if she had and that was true. She said I was good to April so she thought maybe Leo had changed. Stories like that started coming out of the woodwork. Everyone wanted to tell me what kind of man Leo was now. Why hadn't they been more adamant about keeping me away from him before I jumped all over him? Yeah, I wasn't listening and that's the problem. When you're "in love" you can be so blinded to everything else.

The attorney sent me the file and transcript after court. I read it but when I saw what Sarena looked like when they found her suddenly everything clicked. He did it. The argument about child support, the cell phone records, everything. The whole conversation of him telling me we would be alright now. He was convicted, charged, and sentenced to life without parole.

Prison Wife

About two weeks after my family had kidnapped me, I remember his sister calling and asking me if I had left her brother. She asked if I was planning to come back and I told her I would not be back. I stayed true to that, even though I continued being married to Leo, I wanted nothing to do with Clarksdale, Mississippi. Leo was convicted in 2009. At the time of his conviction his mother had cancer but, I'm convinced she died from a broken heart. She couldn't bear to live with the fact that her only son would stay in prison for life. She passed away in January 2011 so I decided to visit Leo while I went to her funeral.

I'm not sure why I finally decided to see him but I was adamant to get down there and see him. After going through that, I never want to visit anyone in prison ever again. The whole experience was dehumanizing. They loaded up the visitors on a bus, then a female officer went through my hair then had me open my bra then my pants to make sure I didn't have anything on me.

After that, we got on another bus that took me to Leo's section of the prison. They had a gathering room with basketball hoops and tables to sit at. Some folks were kissing. I brought Lenny and he ran across the room to hug his daddy. I didn't like it one bit but this was going to be my life. I was a prison wife now. I was told Leo could eventually earn weekend passes so I could come stay with him for a few nights in "cabins" at the prison.

The next day, I was supposed to have a conjugal visit. When I got there, I still had my Mississippi driver's license and they said my ID didn't match my residency. The warden said, "We'll let you visit him but you don't get to go to the room." I am a thousand percent convinced that was the Lord intervening on my behalf thank you, Jesus.

This was my opportunity to finally ask him what had been bouncing around in my mind for the past two years. "Did you kill Sarena?"

Of course, he replied, "No."

I knew he had done it. I'd seen all the evidence against him but for some reason I wanted him to tell me the truth. I wanted to know what had happened that he decided to kill her. I wanted him to tell me so badly, but it never happened. I told him he was a liar and we were through. Then I went back to Seattle and filed for divorce. He refused to sign the paper until February 2012.

The Dating Scene

Even though I wasn't yet divorced, I was going through the healing process and wanted to start dating. I dated a bunch of random men but nothing seemed to work. I just wanted to move on from the fact that I had been married to a lunatic. Surely there was a good man out there somewhere. Then in 2012, God spoke to me so loudly, "Before I bless you with a good man, and a good husband, and a good father for your child; I want you to rededicate your life to me." Then, he went on to say, "I want you to write down the characteristics you want your husband to have."

I was like, "Oh boy, this means I have to stop partying, kicking it, smoking weed, and all of it."

I ended up writing down 36 characteristics that day, I can't remember all of them but I do remember some of them:

- I want him to be tall
- Physically fit
- Handsome
- Must be saved
- Have the Holy Ghost
- Loves his family
- Loves my family
- It's ok if he has kids.
- Ok if he's an ex-con (I think I wrote this down for two reasons, I didn't want to limit myself and deep down

I was always drawn to bad boys but this one had to be saved.)

- Must be employed
- He has to love my child

And the main characteristic above everything else was that he had to love God more than he loved me. I clearly remember asking that. Writing down these characteristics was a lot easier than the first request God presented me—to give my life to him. I was raised Pentecostal; you're supposed to want to live a holy and clean life separated from sin. But I had no idea what that meant for me. Would I have to stop all the fun? No more partying, drinking, or doing as I please? Would I lose my friends? Would I have to become a nun or missionary? I knew one thing, whomever this guy was that God was bringing along, I didn't want him to be a pastor. It wasn't on my list but growing up as a Preacher's kid and living in a fishbowl, was bad enough. I knew I wasn't perfect; I didn't need someone calling my mama or worse my future husband. I thought maybe I could make a bargain with God and give up some things but he spoke to my heart once more and said, "No, Jackie, you need to be all in."

> "Take delight in the Lord, and he will give you the desires of your heart." Psalm 37:4

I began quoting to myself Psalm 37:4 every day. I needed to get this truth inside of me. God wasn't trying to take all the fun out of my life. He was trying to give me a freedom and joy I could never experience from partying and turning it up. It didn't happen overnight; it was a process. I started limiting the alcohol and marijuana. I asked God to take away the taste and desire to smoke cigarettes from me. That one I was able to quit in two days because he fulfilled my desire to quit. I began really building my relationship with God. I started praying daily, reading my word, and worshiping him.

Hart & Boles

It was around the first week of March when I met Chris. I saw him sitting across the room and didn't realize that I knew him until I walked over to him. I had known him all my life; our grandparents had been friends. The thought crossed my mind, *Hey, Chris, is pretty fine maybe you should think about dating Chris.* I cancelled that as soon as it crossed my mind. He was heavily involved with the church, there was no way I'd be able to keep up with him. This man is completely sold out for God, he's...too *holy* to date me. As I was talking to him, I found out that he was going through a divorce. Mine had finalized a month ago but in that moment, I threw Chris out altogether, there was NO WAY I was going to date a married man.

Chris asked if we could get together and talk. He wasn't looking to date; he just wanted a friend to talk to. So, we talked and it was great. I'd never been with a man who didn't want something from me. Chris just wanted to get to know me, he had no motives. We would talk on the phone for hours and even fall asleep on the phone like we were teenagers. We'd talk all the time, any time of day. It was so refreshing to have a person that wanted to get to know me for real.

The first time we went out together, I decided I was going to test him. Anyone can say they are a godly man but I wanted to know if he was for real. I took him to a Kevin Hart show. He had no idea what to wear because apparently all he had were church clothes. I found out later that he had called his dad and his dad told him to run over to Walmart and get some jeans and a t-shirt. So, he did. When we got there, I said, "I'm going to get something to drink. Do you want something?"

"No, I told you I don't drink."

He passed the test and I got my glass of wine. The show was good and we went to Applebee's afterwards. In June, I was turning 40 and my girlfriends flew into town to throw me a big ol' party. I was only able to drink one glass of wine that night, anything else just tasted nasty. I invited Chris to join us but he wouldn't come.

"I can't come to your party, it's at a nightclub. I'm an elder at the church, it wouldn't be right for me to go to a nightclub."

The next morning at church he walked up to me and said, "I'm here to celebrate your birthday with you."

The biggest grin spread across my face. He really did love God and he really did care about me. He wasn't blowing me off by not attending, he was just living out his convictions—wow! Chris even went as far as to ask my parents if he could begin dating me. My father knew he came from a good family so he was all for it but my mother knew his rough background and was a bit more hesitant. She said she would need to think about it because I was her baby and she had to think of Lenny too. My father told my mother it would be ok. I was blown away. I had never had anyone ask my parents for permission to date me and I was a grown woman.

Chapter 14

A GOOD MAN

Finding a good man like Chris after being through the ringer twice was like a breath of fresh air. That's not to say everything was perfect but I was excited to see where things would go and I didn't want to lose him. So, I told God, "You said if I surrendered my will to you, you would bless me. I'm not gonna lose this good man, I want him bad." And at that moment, I put down the liquor, wine, cigarettes, everything.

But before that moment, there were certainly hurdles we faced in the dating process. Chris was a convicted felon. He'd lived the street life and so when he turned things over to God he wasn't playing. His ex-wife had told him that he needed to choose, they could go back to living the streets together or he could do the church thing alone. He chose God and they got a divorce. Then he runs into me. He starts letting his guard down but soon realizes I'm still playing both sides. We met each other like two burned victims, everything was sensitive and uncertain.

There was this one time I had invited him over to my parent's house for a barbeque. All my siblings, aunts, uncles, and cousins were there having a good time. I walked downstairs, ready to make up some margaritas. When Chris found me downstairs making drinks he flipped out. "What are you doing?"

"I'm making drinks."

"This won't work for me." he stormed out of the house, got in his car, but couldn't leave. His car was blocked in so he just sat in his car. (I didn't realize that he was struggling during this time.) I thought he had everything together. He was such a good godly man. I never realized my drinking could be triggering stuff from his past.

> "I was going through a lot of emotions during that time. Jealously, part of me just wanted to party with her, but I knew that wouldn't be good. Distrust, I felt like she was leading me on, was she a church woman or not?" –Chris

I walked out to his car and asked, "Are you really going to leave because I'm making margaritas?"

He said, "Yes, this is not the lifestyle I want."

I had no idea at the time how hard it was for him to tell me this. He really truly wanted to be with me but he knew that he could not compromise even a little. If it came down to it, he would choose God over me. This man was the real deal, he was really serious in his commitment to Christ. It made me want to change things, cause like I said, I didn't want to lose him. I knew he was a keeper! Little did I know that he began to pray for my full deliverance. He had already tried to change women in his life and had gotten nowhere, God was his only hope for me.

A trip to Vegas with some friends was probably one of the most trying experiences in our relationship. When I'd call to talk with him, he'd get kind of snippy with me on the phone. My girlfriends and I had rented a place and we were out there having a good time together. I was excited to talk to him about our plans. "We're getting dressed and going out on the strip."

He dryly replied, "Oh sure you are."

His response threw me off. "What? Are you jealous?"

The truth was that he missed me like crazy. But he had it set in his mind that if he told me, he missed me that would come across as desperate, and his past experiences said women didn't like desperate men, they like tough guys. Deep down he thought I was playing the same game his women in the past had played so he unintentionally fell right into suit and played it back. All the while, he had no idea I was simply talking with him. I wasn't trying to make him jealous of my trip. I just wanted to include him in the experience.

> "I realized that this was a choice. Just because I had been through what I'd been through didn't mean happiness was over for me. God had the power to turn it around. Certain events would trigger something in my past and I'd be willing to walk away from somebody who I knew was a good woman all because of fear. But perfect love casts out fear." –Chris

During that trip, he went quiet for a while. He wouldn't reply to my text messages or answer my calls because of this game he thought we were playing. Here I am, completely oblivious to it. I'm actually kind of hurt and confused, he said he wanted to talk to me but he won't talk to me. So, then I'm wondering but trying not to wonder, what he's up to that he doesn't want to talk to me about.

It's a dangerous game for couples to play and it's always driven by one thing—fear. Fear to lose the person, fear to be honest and vulnerable, and fear to come across as needy. There's not really any point to dating if you don't have the end goal of marriage in mind. If that's not the case then you're both leading each other on. In saying this, the dating period should be where you start to develop some of those communication skills. You've got to talk through things, work through things, and be honest with one another.

Will You Marry Me?

I loved spending time with him because he always treated me like his queen. Even though I had grown up in Seattle he took me to a lot of places I had never been, all of the tourist kind of stuff and we had a blast. We stopped by my parent's house one night before we headed out for a fancy dinner. He had told me to dress up real nice. When we stopped there my mom told me I should take one of her wraps so I wouldn't get cold. We got down to this gorgeous restaurant on the waterfront and as we were sitting at our table, he suddenly gets down on one knee. I noticed the waitress had his phone and was taking pictures.

"What are you doing?"

He started telling me how much he loved me and how he knew he wanted me to be his wife from the moment he saw me. He promised that he would never hurt me, disappoint me, or ever make me feel any type of way ever jealous or anything like that. He had five children and he reassured me that I would never have any baby mama drama. He knew my past and knew that was a sore place for me—ex-girlfriends and baby mama drama. Then he asked me if I would marry him.

I said yes. I'm so beyond happy I'm crying. Everybody in the restaurant is cheering and clapping. Rose petals were all over the floor. It was so beautiful.

The Wedding

We decided to go into planning mode. Would we have a big wedding or a small wedding? Where would it be, who would be in it? We decided to have a maid of honor and best man. He suggested we get married the following month but I asked him to at least give me six weeks to get things together. He only had contact with three of his five children, since he had a lifetime restraining order against the mother of the other two. They had it against each other because their relationship had been very volatile. One of the three was a baby so he was too little to be in the wedding but his son could be a miniature groomsman, his daughter would be the flower girl, and Lenny would be the ring bearer. We knew we were getting into a blended family and we wanted the kids to be a part of this event.

We set the date for September 1st, 2012 and planned for an outdoor wedding at the park. As we're going through all these wedding plans, he begins to tell me that he wants to be a pastor. I began thinking, *God, I told you I didn't want to marry a pastor. What are you doing here?* Chris had hit all the other 36 characteristics I had placed on my list. I suppose it was my own fault I didn't list that out as one. I'm sure God got a little snicker over the whole ordeal. Chris decided he wanted to open up the church August 19th but he wanted to be married first. We decided to have a small ceremony at my parent's house on August 18th. And that became our actual wedding day, August 18, 2012. We got married on Saturday and opened the church on Sunday, that was our honeymoon. I'm not only a wife, I'm a pastor's wife, and we've got church members. I had to laugh, "Oh, God, you are hilarious. You said you would give me the desires of my heart but you didn't say it was going to be like this."

We kept the wedding ceremony we had set for September and after the ceremony we told everyone we had already been married for a few weeks. Most of our close family knew but some people were surprised. It was such a beautiful day. But there were some complications. Three days before the wedding ceremony his ex-wife said she was going out of town and he would need to keep the kids after the wedding. Chris, true to his promise, was not about to let any baby mama drama ruin things. He told her we'd be going on our honeymoon and she'd have to take the kids or he could ask his mom to watch them. We'd already made arrangements for Lenny to stay with my parents.

She said that wasn't going to work because his daughter thought his mother's house was boring. If he didn't want the kids to stay with us after the ceremony then they wouldn't be in the wedding. To my surprise and delight, he replied, "I guess they won't be in the wedding then." I worked at a daycare and had tons of family so it wasn't difficult finding a little girl with the same measurements and shoe size to stand in for the flower girl.

Although I know it disappointed Chris that she chose to be that way, I was thankful to see him react this way right from the start. He really wasn't about to let any baby mama drama come in between us. That spoke volumes to me.

Chapter 15

The Lessons Along the Way

When you enter a relationship with baggage, it takes some time to sort through all the contents of your luggage. Big things, little things. Everything needs to be brought out in the open and addressed at some point. One of the things we had to address was women. Not necessarily the ex-s because that was a drama he was alert to. But all of his "groupies". He was going to a different church than me and had no idea that he had a huge selection of women to choose from.

> *Chris: Well, I had gotten married at a young age and spent a good amount of time in prison so I never really had female friends. You just stay away from them once you're in a relationship because being around them will only cause jealousy. Jackie kept trying to tell me that I needed to be careful because all these women at my church liked me. I didn't want these women; I had no*

> *intentions in my mind of anything like that so I thought she was just being jealous. She kept telling me I needed to be careful with these women.*

This man was oblivious that he had this fan club of women practically throwing themselves at him. He thought they wanted to hear him preach and I was like, oh no, they want more than that, trust me. No married woman calls a single man just because she wants to talk with him. Women know women. I could see what these women were up to and I didn't want his name to be tainted. I knew that it wouldn't matter if he fell or not, just the image alone could destroy everything God was anointing him to do.

When we went public with our relationship, people started coming out of the woodwork to destroy it. People would watch my house just to see if he stayed there all night long, he never did but they wanted something against him. There was even one of my friends who called me up before the wedding and took her time in telling me why I shouldn't marry Chris. "Girl, I'm going to be honest with you because you know you're my girl. You shouldn't marry Chris; he's had three other women."

She even went as far as to tell me that her pastor was going to call me and tell me how horrible of a man Chris was. I never got a call from her pastor. I thanked her for her call but assured her that I loved him and was committed to him. When I called Chris to tell him what she'd said he laughed. Come to find out, she had been trying to date him for a while and he had turned her down. I suppose this was her way of trying to get back at him.

On top of that, people kept trying to tell me about his past, about his record. I guess they thought we didn't talk about these things.

Protect Your Woman

> *Chris: All this craziness brought me to the conclusion that I needed to protect her. Jackie was right and she had been trying to protect me all along, she had recognized things I hadn't. I needed this woman's help in my life. I told her that she needed to promise me she would teach me how to love her the right way. If I was doing something wrong, I needed her to talk with me about it and not just up and leave me. I'd never done this in my past relationships so it was a big part of my healing. All too often men don't want to be told they are doing things wrong. Proverbs 21:9 says, "Better to live on a corner of the roof than share a house with a quarrelsome wife." Even King Solomon knew that nobody wanted a nagging wife. BUT every husband needs a wife who is willing to help him grow and mature. That is a good wife.*

From my perspective, Chris was the stronger one in our relationship. I'll admit I had him on somewhat of a holy pedestal. I just thought he was this amazing God-fearing man who stayed away from alcohol and wouldn't turn up. I admire that about him but had no idea how difficult it was for him to keep his distance from me while I was doing these things. Even more so was my family. My sister, Angie made it clear from the start that she didn't like him because she didn't know him. And of course, my mother had her reservations. I had no idea how difficult this made things for him. He had come out of a relationship where the family didn't like him so he wasn't too excited to jump into a similar situation but he knew he wanted me. And he did everything he could to protect me even from my own self and family.

> *Chris: I remember going to this fashion show with Jackie and some of her family. There were women everywhere. I felt like this was my make it or break it moment with her family. They were testing me to see what kind of a man I was. I spent the entire show staring at the ground or looking up at the ceiling. I couldn't even enjoy the two-hour show because I was so afraid someone in her family might see me looking at one of these models and put the wrong idea in Jackie's head about me. When the show was over her Aunt said, "Jackie, he really loves you. He didn't look at one woman." I think pressure from the family is one of the worst things for men. It can be the end of a relationship in some cases. It makes it worse if the woman allows her family to dictate and meddle in the relationship. Jackie didn't seem to allow that and it helped me to trust her more.*

I remember my sister telling me that I didn't even bring Chris around so she could get to know him before we got serious and got married. Yep, she was right, because I didn't want their opinion. I already knew he was truly a good man so I didn't need them picking him apart and finding stuff to complain about. I just wanted to enjoy him.

Manipulation and Control

I had mentioned Chris shutting down the drama surrounding the wedding ceremony. It didn't take long for me to realize that was how he was, he wasn't about to entertain any obvious drama. A few weeks after the wedding ceremony, his daughter and son wanted to come over to the house. We had bought Lenny a dog and his daughter freaked out. She started screaming and crying, "I'm scared of the dog."

I know some parents might have thought to put the dog up but Chris didn't play that game. He was wiser, he could see that it wasn't his daughter he was dealing with. When you come to my house, you do what we do. His son was fine with the dog but she continued to freak out so he told her she could call her mother to pick her up but we wouldn't be putting the dog up.

His ex- was furious. "You put a dog before our children."

"The dog is part of our family so if you can't see that then I don't know what to tell you."

This happened in October and we didn't hear from them for quite a while. Then, in November, she started warming up to her daddy right before her birthday. I will say, it took us quite a while to pick up on this one. This was his only daughter so Chris had no problems going all out for her but we soon realized she was only seeking him out when she wanted something. The communication would go silent for quite a while then it would always pick back up around the time for school supplies, her birthday, and Christmas.

We'd call and ask why we hadn't heard from her and her mom would always say things had just been busy. Her mom was no different. She'd always start being nice around these events. One day, she called and asked Chris for $1500 to remodel their daughter's bedroom.

"$1500? Why would I give you that kind of money to remodel her room at your house? She has a room here at our house and I have furnished that. And, I haven't even bought my wife a bed, I'm not giving you that money."

He was pretty shocked she had even asked for such a thing. She pitched such a fit over that whole ordeal. Chris was receiving a Citizen's Award from the city for his efforts against gangs and violence. He was ministering to kids on the street and trying to show them if he could get away from the life they could too. It was a big deal on Facebook and she decided to post a comment saying they had no idea who he was, he was someone who wouldn't even take care of his children.

I called her up after that, "Listen, we've always gotten along. We've always respected each other and now you're doing this? I wouldn't even call you but you took it too far. What is the real issue here?"

She said, "I want more child support."

"He's not paying you anymore. You are treated way better than the other mamas, he ONLY gives them child support. We go all out for your daughter's birthdays and Christmas. We help out with things aside from just giving you child support."

Generational Curse

We wouldn't hear from her unless she wanted something, and when she wanted something there would be hell to pay when we said no. But Chris wouldn't budge. He could see what was happening and he wasn't going to allow it to continue. The worst part was that the same behavior his ex was displaying was now showing itself through his daughter.

When she was 12 or 13, she got her own cell phone. We hadn't heard from them for about six months after the bed fiasco, but here she was calling him up asking her daddy to get her an iPhone. He refused to get her a new phone because she wasn't even on his service plan. Things went silent until right before Christmas then she was back again with a smile on her face. He had finally had enough. "I see what this is. If I don't give you what you want then you're going to cut me off and I won't hear from you? I've been a good father; we've had a good relationship but I'm not going to play this game of 'if I don't do what you want me to do then I can't see you.'"

I know it took a lot of strength for him to say that to his daughter. He wanted to continue seeing her but since she only wanted what he could give her he had to put an end to it. It's actually a really great parallel of God's relationship with us. He wants to bless his children but when they start loving the blessings more than the Father he says, "Enough is enough, you've missed the point."

Unfortunately, the same kind of attributes began to develop in his oldest son. His biological mother had run off when he was little so his daughter's mother raised him as her son until his biological mother came back into the picture somewhere in his teens and convinced him to move to Georgia with her. We didn't hear from him for three or four years then suddenly he was reaching out asking us to Cash App him some money. He only needed $10. But come to find out he had also contacted Chris's parents and his sister and asked each of them for $10 as well. Once we recognized the pattern my husband shut it down. He called my husband and cussed him out, calling him all kinds of names. My husband cut him off and told him he wouldn't be disrespected like that.

His son resurfaced again after his biological mother died. He was around 20 or 21. Once again he was back asking for money and once again my husband shut him down. His son became furious and told my husband he was dead to him. My husband said if that was how he felt then he shouldn't contact him anymore.

Blended Family

Being a part of a blended family has had many challenges that we've had to face but we've always stood against them together. We had to or it would have divided us. If I would have said, "Oh babe, you don't really need to cut him off." Who knows what we might have allowed into our marriage? It only takes the smallest foothold for the enemy to wreak havoc. Chris was always good at recognizing and shutting down game-playing and manipulation. He takes great pride in avoiding chaos. Within the church, we call it seeing the devil for who he is or avoiding the enemy and recognizing the enemy. The scripture makes it very clear when it tells us to "Reject every kind of evil." (1 Thessalonians 5:22)

> "Submit yourselves, then, to God. Resist the devil, and he will flee from you." James 4:7

People don't often think about the enemy using those closest to us to bring us down. And yet Jesus rebuked Peter saying, "Get behind me Satan" when he spoke against the will of God. (Matthew 16:23) The enemy will certainly use whomever he can to throw you off of your mission. He was using his son to push my husband's buttons. He wanted to get a reaction out of him by calling him a deadbeat dad and cussing him out. Every person needs to be on alert for this kind of behavior but especially blended families. Don't allow the enemy to control and manipulate you through anyone.

Chapter 16

That's Why She Stayed

As I mentioned in the introduction, I can't speak for all women but I had many reasons why I stayed in both abusive relationships. I've recognized that I'm not the only woman out there who has stayed or is staying for these same reasons.

She Was Wounded

This one doesn't take much explaining. After Mark, I never took time to evaluate myself or allow myself to heal. I simply threw myself at the next man who showed me interest. Which is a dangerous game to play.

She Was Sheltered & Naïve

God said it all the way back in Hosea's time that his people were dying for lack of knowledge. Their lack of knowledge back then and our lack of knowledge is a bit different but, God's words still hold true. Knowledge is power, especially over the enemy. (Hosea 4:6) Which is why a sheltered, naïve woman is the enemy's playground.

Webster's dictionary defines naïve as: marked by unaffected (not influenced or changed) simplicity.

With Mark, I was pretty sheltered. I didn't know much about signs to look for in a user. Aluminum foil around the house and in the car never tipped me off to his abuse because it's not a world I was aware of. Another element which came into play with both relationships was my "unaffected simplicity," I was flat out naïve. I thought every man treated his wife like my father. I couldn't fault Mark or Leo for not measuring up to those standards, maybe they simply hadn't learned them yet. Maybe it was something that came with time.

My head was so full of fairy tale ideals that I couldn't accept the truth when it was staring me in the face. The best way to help women from falling into this trap is to come alongside them, befriend them, and kindly educate them. It's good to know the facts of life and it's good to have some street knowledge. That doesn't necessarily mean you have to live the streets to gain this knowledge either. There are Christians who have come out of rough experiences. Their testimonies need to be shared to strengthen the body of Christ.

Don't hand your past over to the enemy by writing it off and saying it's too shameful to be useful. God didn't do that with David or Paul. They had a lot of shameful events in their past.

As John said in Revelation 1, "We overcome by the blood of the Lamb and the word of our testimony." Don't be ashamed to say, "Yeah, I have a mess of a past but let me tell you about my God who cleaned it up."

She Was Prideful

This one is painful to admit. There was a lot of pride involved with why I continued to stay, regular and religious. I'd grown up in church, we didn't believe in divorce. I even mentioned my pastor telling me that God was going to see me through my marriage with Leo. Obviously, he was not a prophet. The world views marriage as a ball and chain. This is not how God intended it to be at all. He intended for it to be something beautiful. Too many times, Christian women find themselves staying because they're so concerned of what people in the church might think of them for leaving.

The other side of it was the fact that I had come from a privileged family. I had always been successful in whatever I put my mind to. For this reason, I refused to surrender or back down from my first marriage. I didn't want to lose face. What I didn't realize was in the past I only had to worry about myself when I was working hard to achieve goals. Within the marriage, I couldn't do this task alone. We both had to work towards the same goals or we were never going to get anywhere. I was too prideful and stubborn to admit that I was going at it all alone.

She Was Afraid

This is especially true in physically abusive relationships, even more so when there are children involved. Fear has a way of caging us in and causing us to shut down our will to fight. When a gun is held in your face and you're told you'll be dumped somewhere no one will find you, it has a way of keeping you in place. But with God we can be empowered not to find ourselves as slaves to fear. Once this happens, it allows us to seek help.

She Lacked Support

There are many, many reasons why women choose to stay but this has to be the biggest one of them all. When a woman feels that she is all alone she will stay with her abuser just to fulfill the stability he provides even if it is only any illusion. "I don't want to be alone; I don't have the finances to support myself; I don't have a place to stay." These are all things that were going through my mind as I continued on in my relationships.

Be Empowered

My goal in telling you this crazy mess of a story is not to tickle your ear or air my dirty laundry. My hope is that others can use my story and what I went through to be empowered to live their lives. If they are in an abusive relationship then I pray they can seek help in whatever form that may be. If their relationship is great, like my wonderful 9-year marriage to Chris, then I pray they will be on the lookout for people in need. Maybe they can become the support someone needs to wake up and start living in freedom.

Biography of Jacqualine S Boles, RN, MSN

Jacqualine Savanna Boles is a native of Seattle, Wa. A 1990 graduate of James A. Garfield High School in Seattle, Wa., a 1994 graduate of Hampton University in Hampton, Virginia, and a 1999 graduate of Seattle University in Seattle, Wa. She holds a Bachelor and Masters of Science Degrees in Nursing. She is a Certified Family Nurse Practitioner working with the Tiny Tots Development Center, an Early Learning Center that her mother founded in 1969. She is currently the Director of Family and Health Services and focuses on children with Special Needs.

Jacqualine has a wealth of experience in the medical and nursing field. She has worked in most every area of healthcare, including but not limited to emergency, family practice, home health care, school nursing, geriatrics, surgery and her most recent accomplishment natural medicine and plastic surgery.

In 2008 Mrs. Boles experienced a traumatic experience where she almost lost her life due to domestic violence. This event woke up a passion in her pushing her to help educate the world related to Trauma Informed Care. She loves being an advocate for others and a counselor for families and children. She has since founded ***The Jacqualine Boles Consulting Firm***, she focuses on Training, Coaching, Mentoring and Domestic Violence Advocacy.

Jacqualine is an active member of Zeta Phi Beta Sorority, Inc. and has held numerous positions in leadership in this organization. She is also a member of the Mary Mahoney Nurses Association, (Seattle Chapter), The American Nurses Association, and the National Black Nurses Association. She has received numerous award and honors for her years of service to her community at large.

Mrs. Boles is the daughter of the late Bishop James E. Hicks and the late Missionary Helen B. Hicks, Founders of the Unity Church of God In Christ. Her parents are a great inspiration to her life. She is married to Dr. Lawrence Christopher Boles, III and she is the proud mother of 1 son, Freddie Christopher Boles.

Mrs. Boles is thankful for the many years of nursing, and the trials she has experienced enhancing her ability to give in so many ways to our world.